PENGUIN BOOKS
K.L. SAIGAL

Pran Nevile was born in Lahore and took his postgraduate degree from there. After a distinguished career in the Indian Foreign Service and the United Nations, he became a freelance writer specializing in the study of the social and cultural history of India. His particular fascination with the performing arts inspired him to spend many years researching in libraries and museums in the UK and USA.

Nevile has written extensively on Indian art and culture and also acted as a consultant for two BBC films on the Raj. He is the author of *Lahore: A Sentimental Journey, Love Stories from the Raj, Beyond the Veil: Indian Women in the Raj, Rare Glimpses of the Raj, Stories from the Raj: Sahibs, Memsahibs and Others, K.L. Saigal: Immortal Singer, Marvels of Indian Painting, Nautch Girls of the Raj* and *The Tribune—An Anthology 1881–2006* and *Sahibs' India: Vignettes of the Raj.*

K.L. Saigal
The Definitive Biography

PRAN NEVILE

PENGUIN BOOKS
An imprint of Penguin Random House

PENGUIN BOOKS

USA | Canada | UK | Ireland | Australia
New Zealand | India | South Africa | China | Singapore

Penguin Books is part of the Penguin Random House group of companies
whose addresses can be found at global.penguinrandomhouse.com

Published by Penguin Random House India Pvt. Ltd
4th Floor, Capital Tower 1, MG Road,
Gurugram 122 002, Haryana, India

First published by Penguin Books India 2011

10 9 8 7 6 5 4 3 2

ISBN 9780143414063

Typeset in Sabon MT by Eleven Arts, Delhi
Printed at Repro India Limited

www.penguin.co.in

This is a legitimate digitally printed version of the book and therefore might not
have certain extra finishing on the cover.

*For all those
who love to hear
K.L. Saigal*

Contents

K.L. Saigal

K.L. Saigal
(For my father—Ashraf)

Nostalgic for my father's youth,
I make you return
His wasted generation
You felt it all;
the ruined boys echoed through you,
Switched their sorrow on the radio;
the needle turned to your legend.
The wireless sucked your mad notes,
your drunkenness.
You sang them to a sleep of Time
and died.
Counting the ruins of decades,
the boys were left,
caressed with the air's delirium.

—Agha Shahid Ali

K.L. Saigal—
The Perfect Artiste

Aisa koyee fankaar-e-mukammal nahin aaya
Nagmon ka barasta hua badal nahin aaya
Mausiquee ke maahir bahut aaye hain lekin
Duniya mein koyee doosara Saigal nahin aaya.

(A perfect artiste like Saigal, a cloud bursting with melodies, has yet to
be seen again. Many maestros of music have appeared on the scene but
no one has been able to match Saigal.)

—Naushad

Author's Note

K.L. Saigal's music is now a part of our heritage. More than half a century has passed since his premature death in 1947, but the legendary singer's voice endures. One hears from old Saigal fans how he was idolized as the 'Tansen' of his times. There was an aura of mystery about him and, like a snake charmer, he would cause listeners to sway to the sound of his voice. The elemental force of his music stunned the great music maestros of his time, who were amazed at his instinctive knowledge of the ragas and his voice which had a touch of the divine.

During the last few decades a vast amount of literature on Indian music and its exponents has appeared but there is no mention of K.L. Saigal in any of these publications. The only book which carries a brief chapter on K.L. Saigal is *Down Melody Lane* by Saigal's friend G.N. Joshi, himself a musician and a senior executive with HMV for over thirty years who supervised recordings of leading artistes of his time. No serious study or research has been done so far on the life and times of K.L. Saigal. A solitary publication on him by eminent musicologist the late Raghava R. Menon has only a critical review of Saigal's music.

I hope this book will fill the gap—I have tried to present the multiple facets of K.L. Saigal—the singer, actor, poet, composer and person.

There are very few written records of Saigal's life and his contribution to the music and cinema of his time—no diary, no letters or media interviews are available. I met Saigal's daughter Bina and her husband Mohinder Chopra in 1974 and my association with them continued while they were alive. I was able to gather first-hand information from Bina about her father—the artiste and the person—that she had learnt from her mother Asharani, who died in 1978.

For details about Saigal's career as a singer and superstar, I researched and studied the available cinema literature from the 1930s onwards. I tried to collect every bit of information on Saigal as recorded by his mentors and associates. I came upon several anecdotes about Saigal's life but most of these were hearsay. Here, I would like to thank Mrs Shashi Sondhi, Saigal's niece, who volunteered valuable information about Saigal as a lovable family man, saintly and overflowing with affection for everyone. Thanks are also due to Balbir Sikri, a distant relative of his who is now in his mid-eighties, for throwing light on Saigal's routine in Calcutta where he spent nearly two years (1937–39) as a family guest.

An illustrated coffee-table edition of this book sponsored by the Ministry of Culture, Government of India, was published in 2004 as part of the K.L. Saigal centenary celebrations. This revised edition includes additional material in the text in response to suggestions and comments received by the author from readers.

Introduction

The Indian musical tradition is traced to the chanting of verses from the literature of Vedic times. Indian music, one of the most ancient and essentially melodic in form, has retained its roots through the ages. Sounds follow one another and music emerges as a vehicle of expression of the whole range of human emotions, providing different *rasa*s to listeners.

Indian music is referred to as *sangeeta*, which originally included the performing arts of music, dance and drama. According to mythology, the creation of this three-fold art is attributed to Lord Shiva as Nataraja, whose celestial dance symbolizes an ecstasy of motion and rhythm which holds the universe.

The *Natyashastra*, often described as the fifth Veda, is the oldest and most comprehensive treatise on Indian aesthetics and performing arts. Said to have been commissioned by the supreme lord Brahma, the sage Bharata is believed to have compiled it with text taken from the Rig Veda, songs from the *Sama Veda*, action from the *Yajur Veda* and emotion from the *Atharva Veda*. While Bharata's 100 sons rehearsed for a dance drama to be presented in the court of Indra, lord of the firmament, Bharata realized that the *lasya* dance form could only be performed by women. Thereupon, Brahma created *apsara*s, celestial dancers, who entertained the gods by dancing merrily to the accompaniment of music by *gandharva*s, celestial singers.

Music has universal appeal and represents a celebration of life. The origin of Indian music is recognized by historians and scholars as the most ancient; according to renowned violinist and conductor Yehudi Menuhin, the roots of the music of the world lay in Indian music.

In ancient India, music was interwoven with religion and rituals and closely associated with temples. The twelfth-century poet Jayadeva is considered to have been the first Indian musicologist. He composed the *Geet Govinda*, a series of erotic songs in Sanskrit verse describing the amours of Krishna and Radha. He laid down the compatible *tala*, rhythm, in which each section was to be sung. He would sing verses while his wife, an expert dancer, interpreted them in dance form. This astounding lyrical composition was translated into English by Sir Edwin Arnold and called *The Indian Song of Songs*. After Jayadeva, poet–musicians Chandidas, Vidyapati, Tulsidas, Meera and Surdas carried on this Vaishnavite tradition.

One of the earliest forms of Indian classical music was dhrupad, tracing its origin to the *Sama Veda*. Dhrupad compositions were sung in Sanskrit and in regional languages. The advent of Islam introduced Persian, Arabic and Central Asian elements into Indian classical music. Amir Khusro was the first great Muslim musicologist of India. He wrote, 'Indian music, the fire that burns heart and soul, is superior to the music of any other country.' He invented new ragas and introduced new musical forms like qawwali and tarana. He is also said to have invented the sitar.

The temple dhrupad moved to the royal courts and its compositions became more secular in nature. Akbar's reign marked the golden age of dhrupad. Swami Haridas and his disciple Tansen were essentially dhrupad singers. Later, *khayal gayaki* evolved from dhrupad. This Hindu–Muslim fusion enriched the traditional music with more graceful tones and sustained notes.

After the decline of the Mughal Empire, court music moved to the princely states whose patronage enabled musicians to develop new forms of classical music. The lighter and more emotional lyrical forms of thumri and dadra were devised in the court of Wajid Ali Shah, nawab of Lucknow and legendary patron of performing arts, music and dance.

An enchanting facet of Indian music is its relationship with time and seasons. The twenty-four hours of the day are divided into eight parts, beginning at 6 a.m. Every raga is associated with a specific time of the day. Ragas, like Basant, Bahaar and Malhaar, are also associated with seasons.

The advent of British rule in India had a negative impact on the Indian traditional performing arts; the British regarded them as primitive and

Saigal with Nawab in *President*

monotonous. There was now no official patronage, and even princely patronage began to dry up. Musicians had to rely more and more on public support.

At the beginning of the twentieth century, Indian musical culture was at its lowest ebb. Also, as a result of the anti-nautch campaign sponsored and encouraged by the ruling elite and missionaries, music and dance practitioners were stigmatized. Around this juncture, two great devotees of Indian music, Pandit Vishnu Digambar Paluskar and Pandit Bhatkhande appeared on the scene to revive Indian classical music and remind people of our glorious heritage. Beginning with Lahore in 1901, Pandit Paluskar set up institutions for teaching music, called Gandharava Mahavidyalas, in the major cities. Pandit Bhatkhande on his part devoted himself to compiling on a scientific basis, with written notations, the musical compositions of the masters of recognized *gharana*s, or schools. This ushered in a musical renaissance, and by the early 1920s the educated middle-class was becoming interested in Indian music. A number of music societies were then established, and music conferences and festivals were held in metropolitan cities. This in turn provided a platform for talented and accomplished musicians, who were up to then struggling for a living. Classical music began to be celebrated as an artistic heritage, transcending caste, religion, ethnic and language barriers.

The advent of recording brought an altogether new opening for professional musicians. The invention of the gramophone by Thomas Alva Edison in 1877 brought the dawn of a new era in the world of music. Around 1900 Emile Berliner introduced flat discs for recording and since then millions of records have been produced by gramophone companies all over the world. The first recording of an Indian voice was done in 1899 by F.W. Gaisberg in a gramophone company studio at London. The old catalogue mentions the names of the singers as Dr Harnam Das, Dr Bholanath, Hazrat and Ahmed, then living in London. They sang or recited in Persian, Hindi and Urdu, but none of their records have been traced so far.

Recognizing the great potential of this industry in India, the gramophone company set up its office in Calcutta in 1901 and within a year Gaisberg landed in Calcutta with his recording team. In six weeks they travelled to different parts of India and recorded over 600 titles. Most of the artists were professional female singers who had agreed to undergo the special training required for gramophone recording.

The famous Gauhar Jan of Calcutta (1875–1930) was the first artist invited to record by a gramophone company. She belonged to a world of grandeur and refinement, in which the princely durbars and *kotha*s (salons) of *tawaif*s (courtesans) were the hub of performing arts, and was then the most celebrated singer and dancer. Gauhar had learnt music and dance from her early childhood. Her tutors included great maestros of the day, Kalu Ustad of Patiala, Wazir Khan of Rampur, Ali Baksh and Bindadin Maharaj.

Gauhar Jan's maiden public performance in 1887 was before the maharaja of Darbhanga, marking the beginning of her glorious career. For decades before the term Rabindra Sangeet came into use, she sang Tagore songs, dominating the Calcutta entertainment scene. Her gramophone records would conclude with her announcement 'My name is Gauhar Jan.' She recorded over 600 songs during the period 1902–20, contributing in no small measure to the firm foundation of the Gramophone Company in India. She popularized light classical music, including kajri, chaiti, bhajan and tarana, and mastered the technique of rendering a melody in just three and a half minutes. She gained countrywide fame and became a legend in her lifetime. In 1911, she was invited, along with Janki Bai of Allahabad, to sing at the coronation durbar of King George V at Delhi and received a gift of 100 guineas from the Emperor.

Another notable singer of the gramophone era was Master Madan, a child prodigy who is still fondly remembered for his two eternal melodies, *Hairat se taq raha hai jahaan-e-wafa mujhe* and *Yun na reh reh kar humein tarsaiye*. Madan, with his perfectly modulated and unbroken voice, created a sensation in the music world of his time. These two songs were recorded in 1935 when he was only eight. He overshadowed many luminaries of the music world of his day and cast such a spell on his listeners that he was invited to perform by the princely states and the aristocracy who showered gold medals and presents on him. When K.L. Saigal was working in Simla he would often visit Madan's house to meet Mohan, Madan's elder brother, who was also an accomplished musician. Saigal and Mohan would have long singing sessions, with Madan, then only three years old, listening to them attentively. Later, after Saigal had joined New Theatres, he played host to both of them whenever they visited Calcutta. In fact Saigal became very fond of Madan and admired his instinctive knowledge of music and his mastery in singing intricate classical compositions in his heavenly voice with perfect ease.

During the early years, over 500 artistes from all over India were recorded in different languages. The leading ones, besides Gauhar Jan, were Malika Jan of Agra, Janki Bai of Allahabad, Zohra Bai Agrewali, Moujuin Khan and Peara Saheb. Many renowned maestros of classical music, including V.D. Paluskar, Bakhle and Alladiya Khan, refused to be recorded as they thought this would adversely affect the attendance at their concerts.

Abdul Karim Khan (1873–1937) and Inayat Khan were, however, exceptions, but most of the recordings of the gramophone era were done by *baiji*s, professional women singers who received intensive training from the great ustads of their time.

The advent of cinema in 1913, marked by the release of *Raja Harishchandra* which was produced by Dada Saheb Phalke, the founding father of Indian film industry, provided a new opening for musicians. The roaring success of Phalke's first feature film encouraged and inspired many others to venture into film production, and hundreds of silent films were produced during the period 1913–30. Musicians had an important role to play during the screening of silent films. They would be seated in a special pit adjoining the screen stage and would play their harmonium and tabla, providing background music from the foreground. They sang sad or happy melodies to match the movement of scenes on the screen. They would also sometimes say dialogues in a theatrical fashion and sing popular songs to entertain the audience, irrespective of the visuals on screen. The cinema owners even engaged poets to write more effective and meaningful verses to be sung by musicians. Some songs and their tunes captivated the audience and got associated with a particular film and the scene sequence. This heralded the birth of the 'film song'.

Cinema halls presented a lively and amusing scenario. Though films were silent, there would be entertaining sounds all around. Vendors would walk around calling out 'papad, chane, paan-beedi', their goods for sale, in musical tones. The audience on their part enjoyed hooting and whistling during the show. The screening of English films was usually accompanied by piano or violin recitals, or brass bands, as well as popular song numbers for the audience, which largely comprised British soldiers.

The introduction of radio broadcasts in 1927 followed the advent of cinema. This offered another opportunity to musicians, who were invited to give their performances at the studios of radio stations. Originally, broadcasting was undertaken by private operators in Bombay and Calcutta, but in 1930 the government took over radio broadcasting, banning private operators. A substantial part of the broadcast time was allotted to Indian music, apart from Western music and the news in English and regional languages, thus providing a new source of patronage to artistes. The status of a radio singer came to be considered somewhat higher than that of the gramophone one. The prospects of acquiring countrywide name and fame impelled talented musicians to get selected as radio artistes. Interestingly, K.L. Saigal was reportedly rejected after an audition.

The advent of sound with the release of *Alam Ara* (Light of the World) produced in March 1931 by Ardeshir Irani, chief of the Imperial Film Company, brought a revolution in the entertainment scene. Songs and dance now became essential to Indian films. The songs for the first talkies were generally taken from the stage dramas based on classical music, offering fresh opportunities to singers and musicians.

With the phenomenal box-office success of *Alam Ara*, a number of producers rushed into making their 'all talking, singing, dancing' films.

They had to look for new actors and actresses with good voices and diction in Hindi–Urdu. Anglo-Indian actresses, who had dominated the silent era, were replaced by actresses from theatrical companies and professional singing girls who were accomplished in their art and adept at performing in *mehfil*s. Within a couple of months of the release of *Alam Ara*, Madan Theatres of Calcutta, virtually the leaders in Indian cinema, released *Shirin Farhad* and *Laila Majnu*, which became even greater hits than *Alam Ara*. After their spectacular success, Madan Theatres produced eight sound films in 1931 and sixteen in 1932. Their leading stars, Master Nissar and Miss Kajjan, both notable singers, soon became famous in the country. In Bombay, W.M. Khan, Master Bhagwan Das, Ashraf Khan, Gauhar and Zubaida were singing actors.

In those days every actor and actress was expected to sing. The greatest inspiration for cinema was the Parsi theatre and early films were full of songs; *Shirin Farhad* had forty-two songs and *Inder Sabha* had as many as sixty-nine.

The early enthusiasm for song dramas, mythological films, action thrillers and Persian love tales soon wore off and many producers were forced to close shop. Madan Theatres was among them. New producers with fully equipped studios and fresh ideas about social themes entered the field of filmmaking. This hastened the end of musical theatre companies and the film song emerged as the essence and soul of Hindi cinema. The first popular film song was from *Alam Ara—De dey khuda ke naam pe pyare*. It scored more because of its novelty than by merit of its melody.

Cinema houses with single projectors would have a few minutes' interval for changing reels eight or ten times during the show. The audience would sometimes get restless in the dark and would indulge in loud whistling. To mark their appreciation for a song or a dance by the actress on the screen, they would also fling coins on to the stage. With smoking permissible, cigarette smoke hung heavy in the air. The most dramatic moments in a film were those when the action stopped and songs expressed emotions more effectively than the spoken language.

Before the advent of playback singing, singer–actors enjoyed star status in cinema. The popularity of film music is attributed to folk dramas, which had a broad-based history of music that centuries of dramatic tradition had fostered. Another notable feature was the filmic content itself which had been dominated by mythology; music has through

With Uma Shashi in *Chandidas*

the ages been the tongue of mythology in every culture. An important qualification for a singer-actor was a melodious voice and proper accent and diction of Hindi–Urdu words. Even actors who were not good singers, including Sulochana, Devika Rani, Miss Gauhar, Madhuri, Durga Khote, Ashok Kumar and Motilal, were made to sing.

New Theatres of Calcutta was the first to set up a proper sound recording studio. It introduced a new style of film music, based on traditional ragas but fused with popular folk tunes. They had some eminent music directors who not only groomed a new class of singers but also offered a new genre of film songs penned by learned lyricists both in Hindi and Urdu as required by the theme and script of the film. Together they produced fantastic music compositions which retained the traditional classical flavour without its complex expression. It is noteworthy that even after over seventy years many of these songs retain their charm.

Under the studio system, music composers, as regular employees of film companies, related their compositions to the films in question. They also tried to tailor their songs to suit the vocal abilities of the singer–actors. It was Roy Chand Boral who set a new trend in film music which became a model for succeeding generations. He was the guru of Pankaj Mullick; both were responsible for grooming K.L. Saigal and shaping his golden voice.

Facilities for recording at the time, with only a single microphone, were limited and the tempo of the sound was kept at a high pitch. It was common to record in empty cinema halls late, after the night show. Singers would usually be accompanied by a fifteen-man orchestra with a variety of musical instruments, including the jaltarang, flute and tabla-tarang. Western instruments were also introduced. Bengal led in this field and New Theatres had a galaxy of eminent singers like K.L. Saigal, Pankaj Mullick, Pahari Sanyal, K.C. Dey, Kanan Devi (also known as Kanan Bala) and Uma Shashi, the shining stars of the 'new trend', who brought popular music to the cinema goers. The young middle-class, unfamiliar with classical music, found film music more entertaining and easy to imitate.

The mid-1930s ushered in the era of the singing stars led by K.L. Saigal. The credit for discovering Saigal for gramophone recording goes to Chandi Babu, a representative of the Hindustan Recording Company. He had the vision to foresee the great sales potential of Saigal's music and concluded a contract with him. The first Saigal record brought out by the Hindustan Recording Company was the unforgettable *Jhulana jhulavo*, which created a sensation with a sale of five lakh records. After this record, Saigal made a contract with the company to sing on a royalty basis. This was new in the music industry as musicians usually sold their songs for a one-time payment of an agreed price. In later years, Saigal's film songs were recorded by the Gramophone Company of India under their HMV label in accordance with their exclusive agreements with film producers. However, all of Saigal's non-film songs were issued under the Hindustan label. The gramophone company got interested in film music only in the mid-1930s and recorded only a few selected songs from the current Hindi films. But as they proved to be very popular, while the sales of non-film classical and regional music declined, the company decided to bring out records of songs of earlier Hindi–Urdu films.

The recording for gramophone discs was undertaken separately at the HMV studios in Calcutta and Bombay after the song recording for the films. Until the introduction of magnetic tape in the 1950s, songs would be recorded twice. Transfering music from the sound track to a

In the role of Tansen at Akbar's court in *Tansen*

gramophone record was not convenient and a disc could typically have fewer songs on it than the soundtrack had.

According to an HMV source, when Saigal appeared for an audition at their Delhi studio and subsequently at their Calcutta rehearsal room, he was rejected at both places for his lack of formal training by the one-man selection committee. No one took notice of the exceptional quality of his voice, his unusual natural talents and instinctive knowledge of classical ragas.

In 1954, B.N. Sircar, anxious to honour the memory of his favourite star K.L. Saigal, managed to make a film biography of Saigal called *Immortal Singer* or *Amar Saigal*. Actor Mungheri was hired to play the role of Saigal but the project flopped. The only attraction of the film was the clippings from Saigal films.

Renowned music director Naushad of *Shah Jehan* fame later elevated K.L. Saigal to the pedestal of Mian Tansen. He said, 'Saigal outdid Tansen in popularity. Mian Tansen was of course the beloved of his times, but his voice was in a way imprisoned in the palace walls—there only for the select upper class. Saigal on the other hand had a whole nation behind him—as he was a music man for the millions. He was in fact their Tansen.'

More than six decades have elapsed since Saigal left us, but his heavenly voice continues to haunt millions of his fans. A great artiste and man, Saigal belonged to the class of people who defied death—he is the immortal singer.

Early Years

K.L. Saigal was born in Jammu on the fourth day of the fourth month of the fourth year of the twentieth century (4 April 1904). His father Amar Chand was a tahsildar in the service of the maharaja of Jammu and Kashmir. A man of reasonably good means, commanding respect in local circles, he had four sons—Ram Lal, Hazari Lal, Kundan Lal and Mohendar Lal. Kundan Lal, universally known as K.L. Saigal, was to earn name and fame as the greatest musical genius of the century.

From his early childhood, Kundan showed an unusual interest in music and picked up ditties and songs from wandering ministrels, temple priests, faqirs and jogis. His father resented Kundan's fondness for music but his mother Kesar Devi, herself an accomplished singer of bhajans and folk songs, encouraged him, believing that he had inherited this gift from her. He would entertain his mother, singing as he did in his unique, melodious voice. The mother–son duo would sing bhajans at *kirtan*s and temple festivals.

At the age of ten, Kundan began taking part in local *Ram Lila* celebrations, playing the role of Sita, a singing heroine, in the scenes of the wedding, banishment, abduction to Lanka, return to Ayodhya and her final merger with Mother Earth. Kundan enjoyed doing the role and waited all year for Dussehra so that he might sing as Lord Rama's virtuous consort. He would be thrilled by the applause he received from the people who liked to hear him singing. The *Ram Lila* celebrations in his area became famous in Jammu.

Saigal's father allowed him to sing at the *Ram Lila* and would attend because of his religious feelings. He was greatly disturbed at the young boy's alarming interest in music and total neglect of his studies. He

Standing from L to R:
K.L. Saigal, family friend, Mohinder Saigal (brother)
Sitting from L to R: Pushpa Saigal (wife of Mohinder), Neena Saigal
(daughter of K.L. Saigal), Asharani Saigal (wife), Kesar Devi (mother) and in
her lap Bina (daughter of K.L. Saigal), sister, niece and family friend.
On the floor: *Madan Mohan Saigal (son).*

tried to check him and even punished him but to no avail. He had other aspirations for his son and was disappointed to see him wandering about, singing all the time, not caring for his unkempt appearance and lack of ambition. Once, as punishment, Kundan was made to work in the kitchen and serve food to everyone in the family. He took it lightly and sang away the rebukes and even the slaps on his face. It might have this early experience in the kitchen which many years later flowered into his well-appreciated culinary expertise. We come across a special mention of it by his cousin Chaman Puri, the brother of the late Madan Puri and Amrish Puri, who said, 'No one in the family cooked mutton like Bhaisaab.'

It is said that when Saigal was a boy of just twelve, he made his historic debut at a court function in the presence of Maharaja Pratap Singh of Jammu and Kashmir, a great connoisseur of music. The young Saigal sang devotional hymns of Meera with such expressiveness and fervour that everybody was wonderstruck.

Kundan had also picked up singing from folk singers. He would sneak away to the vicinity of the house of a singing girl in the neighbourhood and hear her practise in the daytime. Jammu was then known for its generations of famous classical musicians who trained professional singing girls who looked for patronage from the maharaja's court. Ali Baksh, father of Bade Ghulam Ali Khan and ustad of the famous Malika Pukhraj, then lived in Jammu. There were also other musicians for whom Jammu had such a great attraction that they were ready to teach for two meals a day rather than go elsewhere. It is said that Kundan also had a chance to learn something when a local musician was engaged at his home to amuse and soothe his ailing elder brother.

When Kundan was around thirteen years old his voice showed the first signs of breaking. This of course was quite normal, but the young boy got the shock of his life as his soprano suddenly disappeared. Fearing that he might not be able to sing any more, he got terribly upset and lost interest in everything. He became silent and kept to himself, brooding all the time. His family got worried and his mother was especially disturbed as she greatly missed his company when she sang bhajans in the evening.

In those days when many jogis and sufis lived near Jammu; some had their own *dera*s. Free from the shackles of family ties, they were lost in their mystic quest. People had faith in them, and would visit them to seek

K.L. Saigal with his family

their blessings. Some of the sufis and jogis sang the Sufiana Kalam of Hazrat Bulle Shah, the great Punjabi saint, their voices leaving listeners stunned. Among them was Pir Salman Yousuf, a direct descendant of Serajuddin of the Yesevi sect. This pir had blessed Kundan when he was born.

Unable to bear the depression of her son, Kundan's mother took him to the pir. The pir dispelled her fears and prophesied that Kundan would earn great name and fame. Kundan told the pir that he could not survive without singing, and begged him to do something. The pir told him not to lose his heart and to consider that this break in his voice would prove to be the luckiest thing in his life—it would be like a rebirth. He instructed him to stop singing for two years and to start practising and cultivating his voice by *zikr* and *riaz*. Then the pir cautioned him, saying, 'Remember, this is a secret practice. Like the darkness that a seed needs to sprout, this *zikr* and this *riaz* need a secret place in which they sprout. As you grow in this practice you will have made the *swara*s of your music all by yourself and since these are your own *swara*s, the songs you will sing with them will also be yours, your own songs, no matter whose they might have been, before you sang them. Speech and song will become one for you. You will be able to sing anything and remember anything. This *zikr* and this *riaz* can move mountains. The impossible will become possible. But you must not stop this practice any time in your life. *Riaz* and *zikr* are life itself and if you practise, it will become your life far more truly than your life is your own now. I can tell you nothing more. If with this boat you cannot cross the river of your life, I cannot help you. Now get up, dry your eyes and make a resolve in your conscience that for two years from now you will not sing but practise what I have given you. Go in peace.'

Kundan listened to every word spoken by the pir and made a resolve to follow his instructions. Even in later years tuning his *swara* was a constant routine for Saigal. Kundan now emerged as a transformed person with a revived interest in life.

In the following year, his father retired from service and the family moved to their ancestral house in Jullundur, now called Saigal Mohalla, near the Pan Pir gate. Having dropped out of school, Kundan was left with only one pursuit, his passion, music. No one noticed this change in him, and expected him to return to the mundane in due course and 'settle down' in life like other young men of middle-class families. On his part, Saigal realized that it was not what he was cut out for, and that his quest was to understand the mystery and meaning of music. He met Punjabi folk singers in Jullundur and learnt about the traditional ragas integrated into the verses of Punjabi love legends like Waris Shah's *Heer* and *Sohni–Mahiwal*.

At the Har-Vallabh music festival in Jullundur, the annual traditional gathering of musicians from all over India, Saigal had the opportunity to listen to the classical maestros of the day. He keenly observed the vocal styles of the eminent khayal and thumri singers of famous *gharana*s from Lucknow, Banaras, Agra and Gwalior, and he would try to imitate them and then sing in his private gatherings. Saigal was now completely engrossed in his art, more to satisfy his inner urge than to entertain his listeners. He continued with his vigorous *riaz* and imbibed musical skills from every possible source, from sadhus and faqirs to eminent masters of classical music. Not very concerned with the theory of music, he treated music as an essentially practical art. He nurtured his voice with *riaz* and within a span of three to four years, he succeeded in developing it to such a level that it could be compared to the notes emerging from a violin or a sarangi. Also, he was able to control the volume of his voice by manipulating his breath.

As time passed, Saigal felt that he should move away from the restrained atmosphere of his home. He wanted to do something for a living so he could continue his passion for music, which was food for his soul. One day, he left his home without telling anyone in the family where he was going. This was the beginning of his period of wandering, which extended over about eight years.

Saigal never left any diary or record of his reminiscences. There are stories about his taking up all sorts of jobs in different towns and cities, including Lahore, Kanpur, Bareilly, Moradabad, Simla and Delhi. Although he never informed his family about his whereabouts, he kept in touch with his mother, telling her about his well-being.

There is no evidence whatsoever of whether he learnt music from any teacher during this period. It is mentioned that he took a job in the Railways at Lahore and later went to Moradabad and then to Delhi.

Music scholar Raghava Menon gives a detailed account of Saigal's stay in Moradabad, based on his personal meeting with Imtiaz Ahmad, a sarangi player who accompanied local classical singers and also worked as a *unani hakim*. Imtiaz is reported to have heard Kundan, then in his late teens, humming a thumri one afternoon at the deserted railway platform. It was the same thumri which Abdul Karim Khan had sung at a function on the previous day when Imtiaz Ahmed had accompanied the maestro with his sarangi. Imtiaz was captivated by the young Kundan's voice and style of singing, especially the way in which he was trying to reproduce the cadences of the song. He was also struck by the young Kundan's confidence and authority in singing which made the song his own, rather than something he had heard and was trying to imitate.

Imtiaz took the boy home and was surprised when Kundan told him that he had not learnt music from any teacher. He was amazed and asked him to sing something else. Saigal told him that he had learnt some bhajans and ghazals on his own. Then he sang as though 'the words [would] look after the music, sometimes almost speaking the lines booming with the resonance of the note in which he had almost, but not quite, spoken the words one after another.' Later Imtiaz realized that Saigal had not even enquired about the tuning of the sarangi, since he had not had any formal training. But, at the same time, he felt that Saigal was right, for what he did with his music was completely different from what he could have learnt from any kind of training.

The young Saigal probably spent a year or two at Moradabad. Imtiaz also mentioned that the British stationmaster's wife had taught the young Saigal to read, write and speak English. Another episode involving Saigal at Moradabad is told by his great friend and colleague from New Theatres, Pahari Sanyal, who recalls having met him there in September–October 1929. Sanyal was then in Lucknow but often visited Moradabad to participate in musical gatherings. It was on one such occasion that he met the young Saigal who was regaling the audience with his lively songs. He recognized him, having met him earlier in Delhi around 1927. According to another account attributed to Saigal's cousin, actor Madan Puri, Saigal came to Delhi in 1928 in search of a job and stayed with his two Muslim friends, Mohammad Salam and Mohmad Razak, both from Jullundur and working in the Telegraph Office. It is said that Saigal took up a job in the Delhi Electricity Department and that later his brother Ram Lal, who was employed at the Shahdara railway station, got him a time-keeper's job at the Delhi railway station. But after working for a year or so, Saigal, without informing anyone, disappeared.

There is also an account of Saigal being in Simla during this itinerant years. No precise dates are mentioned but, according to his cousin Chaman Puri, when Saigal was in Simla, he ran short of funds and had no money to pay his hotel bills. The only course open to him was to earn

K.L. Saigal

A scene from *Chandidas*

something by singing. He is said to have dressed himself as a pandit-preacher and sang Urdu verses from Pandit Radheysham's *Ramayan ki Katha*. The event got enough publicity just by word of mouth and the hill-people assembled in large numbers to hear him. Saigal collected about 300 rupees as *dakshina* for his discourse lasting a fortnight.

Next, he is believed to have worked as a hotel manager before returning to Delhi. All available evidence points to the fact that Saigal finally landed the job of a travelling salesman with the Remington Typewriter Company at Delhi. It is likely that the attraction of travelling appealed to his restless nature and temperament. He was also obliged to learn to type so he could carry out demonstrations to satisfy the prospective clients.

He continued to live anonymously, not disclosing his whereabouts to his family. Apparently, it was a business trip that took him to Calcutta, where the head office of his company was located. Calcutta was then the cultural hub of the country and the centre of the performing arts. Eminent artistes from all over north India came there for fame and fortune. Many theatrical companies were established there and after the advent of the talkies, a number of film studios appeared on the scene. Calcutta became the mecca for prospective actors, actresses, scriptwriters, lyricists, singers and directors. Saigal was also destined to attain countrywide fame as the king of melody from Calcutta.

In Calcutta

It wasn't his looks, or brains, charm, illustrious lineage or special training from an eminent ustad. But the camera saw in K.L. Saigal a real person—truth personified—and the microphone reverberated with a touch of the Divine.

How did Saigal land in the New Theatres studio at Calcutta? There are three different versions. The first one, by the renowned music director Pankaj Mullick, points to his first meeting with Saigal in 1931 at the Calcutta radio station, then a private concern known as the Indian Broadcasting Company, where Saigal had come for an audition. Pankaj Mullick, who was working as a singer and music trainer, was very impressed by the winsome looks and speech of the young man. Soon after he heard Saigal sing a ghazal, he had Saigal selected as a regular artiste of the company.

New Theatres was then the leading film-production studio of Calcutta. Set up in early 1931 by B.N. Sircar, with the famous elephant logo, it was not only equipped with the latest and best imported sound and photo machinery, but also had the finest talent—directors, music directors, cameramen, scriptwriters, and actors and actresses—in the country. Pankaj Mullick had been connected with New Theatres from its inception as one of its two music directors, the other being the famous R.C. Boral. New Theatres' first talkie was *Dena Paona* (1931), in Bengali, directed by the well-known littérateur Premankur Atorthy. When B.N. Sircar decided to make Hindi versions of the films for an all-India exhibition, he needed an artiste for the role of a singing hero in the films. Pankaj Mullick at once thought of Saigal and introduced him to Atorthy, who with Sircar's approval cast him in the leading role

Chowringhee, Calcutta, c. 1935

of the New Theatres' first Hindi film *Mohabbat ke Ansoo*. The debut was successful beyond expectations and this led to the starring of K.L. Saigal in most of New Theatres' Hindi films that followed.

The second account of Saigal's recruitment in New Theatres is attributed to the illustrious music director R.C. Boral who met Saigal through his friend Harish Chander Bali, a well-known classical singer from Jullundur, who was his regular house guest when he visited Calcutta. Bali had been anxious to find an opening for Saigal in films as he was confident that the young man could make his mark as a singing star. New Theatres in those days took pride in its singers like K.C. Dey and Pankaj Mullick. Bali persuaded Boral to give Saigal a chance and listen to his singing. There was stiff competition in the field as many singer–actors from theatrical companies were unemployed after the advent of the talkies.

One morning Boral met Saigal with Bali and asked him to sing. Saigal began singing almost at once, standing and without any accompaniment. Describing the incident later, Boral could not recall what Saigal sang that day. It might have been in Bhairavi or Asavari, or another morning raga. But Boral was astounded and had felt that a great ustad had been singing. 'It was a bhajan that Saigal had chosen to sing. The voice was sure, very precise, finely focused on the note. He did not seem capable of wasting a particle of his breath, and had a timbre that rang like a *been*, a *been* whose every string had been carefully tuned. Although there was not even a whistle accompanying him, it seemed as though an invisible sarangi was following his every move, prowling about near his notes, nudging him along to elaborate.' Boral spoke to B.N. Sircar about his delightful experience of listening to Saigal and assured him that this young man would be a success in films. Sircar, on his part, left the choice and decision to Boral. So, Saigal joined the talented bunch of New Theatres.

Another version takes us to a *paan* shop at the Esplanade where Saigal was humming *Kaun bujhaye tapat more man ki*. That evening there was another customer who overheard him and was enchanted by the magic of his voice. This person was Hafizjee who took him to the New Theatres' office and persuaded B.N. Sircar to hear him sing. Sircar was so impressed that he at once cast him in his forthcoming film *Mohabbat ke Ansoo* (1932), a romantic drama.

Finally, we have B.N. Sircar reportedly telling Abdul Ali of the Cine Society, Mumbai in December 1978, 'K.L. Saigal was chosen by me some time in November 1930 at a social gathering that had taken place at the betrothal ceremony of a film distributor, Mr Kazi from UP. When I was invited to this event, I had with me Nitin Bose, Hafizjee and, as I did not know much about music, I had taken R.C. Boral with me. We heard him sing at this meet and that led to his joining the New Theatres.'

Before the emergence of New Theatres, the cinema scene in Calcutta was dominated by Madan Theatres, established in 1902 by J.F. Madan, a Parsi theatre-enthusiast. The leading distributor, producer and exhibitor, this company owned in those days 172 cinema houses and earned half the national box-office receipts, besides producing the largest number of silent films. After the advent of the talkies, they had great initial success with their sound films, *Shirin Farhad* and *Laila Majnu*, both romantic musicals with the famous singing duo of Master Nissar and Miss Kajjan. They could not, however, survive the fast-changing entertainment scene and competition from the new rivals. New Theatres launched its film production with new and fresh ideas, doing away with the practice of converting stage dramas into films. The East India Film Company, Bharat Laxmi Pictures, Radha Films, Kali Films and Pioneer Films also set up their studios in Calcutta.

With the phenomenal success of *Alam Ara*, heralding the era of the talkies, many other companies rushed into production, with mythological stories and old popular dramas loaded with songs.

New Theatres followed up its first Urdu film, *Mohabbat ke Ansoo*, with *Zinda Lash*, a comedy, and *Subah ka Sitara*, the romance of a slave girl with an aristocrat, both of which starred Saigal in the leading role and Rattan Bai as the heroine. Neither film made a lasting impression and struggled to just break even. Sircar was quick to realize that the wealth of Bengali literature, of Gurudev Tagore, Bankimchandra Chatterjee, Saratchandra and others, should be explored and stories rooted in Bengali life transcribed onto film for millions to see. In 1932, he succeeded in persuading Gurudev to direct a film version of his dance drama, *Natir Puja*, based on a Buddhist legend. It was a great success all over the country. The same year another success followed, with the release of the Bengali version of *Chandidas* (1932), directed by Debaki Bose, in which he gave a lyrical exposition of Vaishnavite philosophy.

Encouraged by the success of *Chandidas*, Sircar picked up the Punjabi legend of a devotee prince, *Puran Bhakt* (1933). Directed again by Debaki Bose, with enchanting music by R.C. Boral, the film was a box-office hit. K.L. Saigal appeared in the film during his own song sequences. His songs—*Bhajun main to bhav se siri girdhari, Din neekey beetey jaat hain, Avsar beeto jaat prani* and *Radhey rani dey daro na bansari mori*—were greatly appreciated by the cinema audience and contributed in no small way towards the film's resounding success. *Puran Bhakt* was hailed as a masterpiece of the New Theatres by the Punjab Cinema Art Society, which held a special function to honour B.N. Sircar and Debaki Bose at Lahore while the film was running to packed houses at the local Majestic Talkies. Addressing the function, Professor A.S. Bokhari (who later became the director-general of All-India Radio) called Debaki Bose 'a great man' and described *Puran Bhakt* as a landmark in Indian

Singing in *Lagan*

cinema art with its skilful use of background music and wonderful
songs for entertainment. Boral introduced new elements in his music
composition by combining folk forms with classical Indian ragas. This
was later adopted and further refined and embellished by the other
music directors who followed him, like Timir Baran, Pankaj Mullick,
Khemchand Prakash and Ghulam Haidar. Debaki Bose treated the theme
in an artistic and natural way and his new techniques in shooting and
editing set a new trend in the development of Indian film production.
The same year, he also directed *Rajrani Meera*, starring Prithviraj
Kapoor and Durga Khote, on the life of the famous sixteenth-century
poetess-queen and devotee of Lord Krishna, who gave up royal luxury
and became an ascetic, singing and writing some of the most sensuous
poetry in praise of her lord. The music was scored by Boral and Saigal
appeared in a minor role as one of the devotees.

In 1933, New Theatres released *Yahudi ki Ladki*, directed by
Premankur Atorthy with music by R.C. Boral and Pankaj Mullick. The
film was based on Aga Hashar Kashmiri's well-known play *Misar Kumari*,
a favourite subject for the stage. A faithful adaptation of Kashmiri's

Saigal as Prince Marcus in *Yahoodi ki Ladki*

Parsi theatre classic was also staged in Bengali in 1919. The costumed extravaganza was one of the early New Theatres' elaborate productions which were box-office hits, particularly in north India. It was also a musical treat, with Saigal and Rattan Bai in the leading roles. It had the famous Ghalib number *Nuktachin hai gham-e-dil usko sunaye na bane*. Boral's adoption of the ghazal style into the light classical form charged with emotion was remarkably interpreted by his protégé, Saigal.

Ghazal singing was not known to cinema lovers. Saigal introduced to the audience simply worded ghazals like *Maiy mein wo masti kahan, jo tere mastane mein hai*, also from *Yahoodi ki Ladki*. The film, described as New Theatres' mighty spectacle, portrayed a grand and immortal story of love and sacrifice and was acclaimed by the media as one of the best pictures of 1933.

In 1934, New Theatres brought the memorable hit *Chandidas*, a Hindi remake of Debaki Bose's 1932 film. It was directed by photographer Nitin Bose, with music by Boral. Saigal dominated the picture in its title role with heroine Uma Shashi featuring in the popular duet *Prem nagar mein banugi ghar mein* and other songs. Based on the life of the legendary fifteenth-century Bengali poet Chandidas, it portrayed a socially relevant topic by highlighting the evils of untouchability and caste barriers. The theme of universal love was advocated, with the lovers discarding tradition-bound religion. The songs, written by the eminent literary figure, Aga Hashar Kashmiri, and suffused with love and yearning, like *Tadpat beete din rain*, continue to enchant listeners. The stupendous success of the film at the box office brought K.L. Saigal not only all-India fame and popularity but also elevated him to the rank of the foremost star of New Theatres. At the same time, he was acclaimed as the most popular singer, with a voice unmatched by any artiste in the country.

Chandidas was followed by *Rooplekha*, a semi-historical film directed by Pramathesh Chandra Barua, in which Saigal played Emperor Ashoka. After this came the historic super-hit *Devdas* (1935) directed by the creative genius P.C. Barua, with Saigal and Jamuna playing the lead roles. This great classic, based on Saratchandra's literary masterpiece, immortalized New Theatres and set a milestone in the Indian film industry. The film created a sensation and brought a revolution in the film world. It introduced new standards and concepts in the field of film production. It also brought home the important role of cinema in society and its powerful influence on the public mind. A separate chapter is devoted to the study of this all-time great classic.

The film companies of Bombay were more concerned with quantity rather than quality. They were still reproducing mythological dramas, lacklustre remakes of old silent films such as *Gun Sundri*, and action thrillers. They remained aloof from literary sources. One film company, Ajanta Cinetone, however, did engage Munshi Premchand to do a script for *Mazdoor*, with a novel theme of the labour–capital conflict and portraying the exploitation of poor workers. Directed by M. Bhavnani and starring Jairaj and Bibbo, the film had problems with the censors and was a commercial failure. Another company made *Seva Sadan*, based on Premchand's novel but had little success. The famous writer was disappointed with the filmic versions of his works and distanced himself from the Bombay film world. The only upcoming director who made his mark was V. Shantaram of Prabhat Film Company. His classic *Amrit Manthan*, starring Chandramohan and Shanta Apte, was a great box-office hit. The film, with striking new technical features, became a landmark of Indian cinematography of those days.

After *Devdas*, New Theatres released two films, the first of which, *Inqilab*, directed by Debaki Bose, was inspired by the tragic Bihar earthquake and exposed the activities of anti-social elements who exploited the calamity. The second film was the famous hit *Dhoop Chhaon*, directed by Nitin Bose with Boral's lovely music rendered by K.C. Dey. This was the first film in which the technique of playback singing was introduced. Though Saigal had no acting role in the film he sang its popular hit *Andhe ki lathi tu hi hai* for the recording company. Another Saigal film *Karwan-e-Hayat*, directed by P. Atorthy, was an adventure movie where Saigal plays a romantic prince in the guise of a commoner wooing a princess but in the garb of a dancing girl. R.C. Boral gave some lovely songs including an appealing ghazal by Ghalib, *Dil se teri nigah jigar tak utar gayi*. This was followed in 1936 by two Saigal films, *Crorepati* and *Pujarin*. The first was a comedy directed by Hem Chander in which Saigal has the role of a crazy youth who has won a lottery. The film also had other leading stars of New Theatres, such as Pahari Sanyal, Jagdish Sethi, Nawab, Kidar Sharma and Molina, adding humour and colour to the film. *Pujarin* was a remake of New Theatres' first talkie *Dena Paona* (1931, whose most striking feature was Saigal's unforgettable melody *Piye ja, aur piye ja,* perhaps the only song recorded without any rehearsal or full composition. Neither film, though commercially successful, was an all-India hit.

In the meantime, Bombay producers also came out with some popular hits, the most outstanding of which was Bombay Talkies' *Achhut Kanya*, starring Devika Rani and Ashok Kumar, who emerged as a popular pair. As a singer, Ashok Kumar made little impression and the other singer–actor Surendra was dismissed as a poor clone of Saigal. V. Shantaram

With Leela Desai in *President*

A scene from *President*

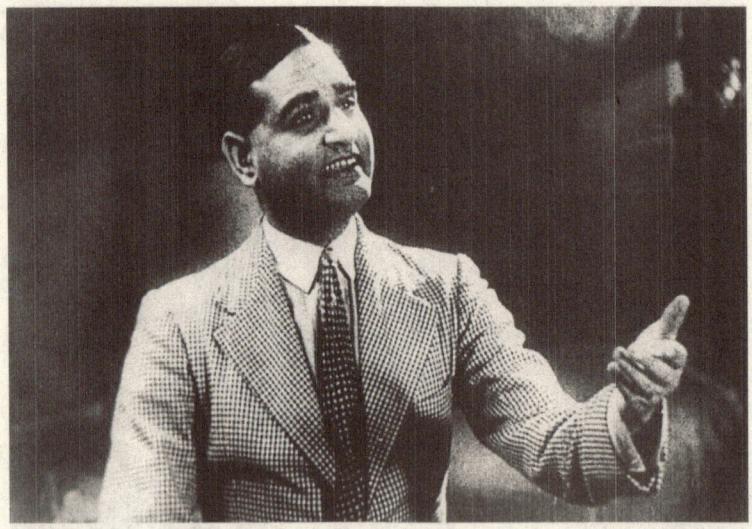

Singing *Ek bangla bane nyara* in *President*

of Prabhat came out with a remarkable adventure classic *Amar Jyoti*, featuring Durga Khote in a memorable role as a pirate queen.

Indian cinema was now maturing and taking note of changing tastes. The appeal of mythology and fantasies was fading, and the educated middle class was looking for more sophisticated entertainment in films; leading filmmakers were looking for new subjects. New Theatres had already established its supremacy and even succeeded in moulding the tastes of the cinema-goers by setting new standards in quality and choice of themes for their films. The year 1937, however, saw a giant leap with V. Shantaram's great classic *Duniya Na Mane*, considered one of the best films made in India. Based on a novel by N.H. Apte, it dealt with the social evil of young maidens being married off to old men; the heroine fights this injustice and the old husband, realizing his impropriety, gives her the freedom to remarry by committing suicide. K. Date and Shanta Apte won laurels for their superb performances in this great hit.

From New Theatres came another Saigal film, *President*, directed by Nitin Bose. The film dealt with a novel theme, presenting an Indian woman as a business chief of a textile mill. The film was an interesting triangular drama with two sisters, played by Kamlesh Kumari and Leela Desai, falling in love with the same man, a talented mill-worker,

In *Dharti Mata*

played by Saigal. He sang some unforgettable songs like *Ek bangla bane nyara* and *Prem ka hai is jag mein panth nirala*. Saigal also sang that famous rhyme where speech turns into a melody as he calls upon the children with *Ao bacho, tumhen aj ek kahani sunain*. The melody *Ek raje ka beta lekar*, with speech interludes, followed. During 1938, New Theatres released two remarkable pictures starring Saigal. The first was *Dharti Mata*, directed by Nitin Bose, with music by Pankaj Mullick and Uma Shashi as the heroine. This was the first film that dealt with the subject of Indian agriculture and the need for modern means for its development. The film is also a love story and Saigal dominated the scenes with his two memorable songs *Kisne ze sab khel rachaya* and *Ab main kah karun kit jaun*.

The second film *Street Singer* was one of the all-time great classics of Indian cinema. For New Theatres, the Saigal–Kanan singing duo surpassed all previous records and the film turned out to be their greatest musical hit. Directed by Phani Majumdar, who regarded Saigal as a greater actor than singer, and with music by R.C. Boral, the film portrays two waifs, Bhulwa (Saigal) and Manju (Kanan), looking for an opening in the theatre world, which the woman gets while the man doesn't. In addition to other songs, Saigal's all-time hit, the haunting thumri *Babul mora naihar chhuto hi jaye* by Wajid Ali Shah, continues to be associated with his memory as an immortal singer. This was followed in 1939 by *Dushman* with the same team but Leela Desai replacing Uma Shashi. Though sponsored by the government to promote the anti-tuberculosis programme launched by the Vicereine Lady Linlithgow, the film was a major hit due chiefly to the creative genius of Nitin Bose and some haunting numbers by Saigal, as well as his marvellous portrayal of a tuberculosis patient in love. Saigal fans fondly remember his hit songs *Karun kya aas niras bhai* and *Preet mein hai jeevan jokhon mein*.

The last year of the third decade was quite eventful in the Bombay film industry as well. Sohrab Modi won laurels for his grand historical *Pukar* depicting an episode in the life of the justice-loving Emperor Jehangir, with Chandarmohan and Naseem Bano in the leading roles. With dazzling sets, costumes and decor, the film set new records in the box office. Bombay Talkies also did not lag behind and came up with a big romantic hit–*Kangan*–with the new pair Ashok Kumar and Leela Chitnis. Another striking film was Prabhat's *Admi*, one of Shantaram's masterpieces, depicting the life and tribulations of a 'fallen woman'. The year also saw, in September, the beginning of the Second World War which was to have far-reaching effects on the film industry in the country.

The war situation created a shortage of many imported materials, including raw film. Producers were forced to economize by reducing the length of films, which in any case were invariably much longer than the English films. During 1940, there was only one film starring Saigal from

Looking pensive in *Jiban Maran* (Bengali)

Singing on the radio in *Jiban Maran*

With Leela Desai in *Jiban Maran*

New Theatres, P.C. Barua's *Zindagi*, another classic which repeated the *Devdas* team with Jamuna as the heroine. Typical of Barua's perception of married life, the film depicts an affair between a young educated jobless youth and a rich married woman who had run away from a bad husband. A highly unconventional theme for those days, the film is remembered for its charming lullaby *Soja raj kumari so ja*. The last film Saigal did for New Theatres before leaving for Bombay in late 1941 was *Lagan*, directed by Nitin Bose. A forerunner of Guru Dutt's *Pyasa* (1956), the film portrays a triangular love drama of a poet, his beloved and her husband. The Saigal–Kanan duo offered many enchanting songs composed by R.C. Boral, such as *Kahe ko raad machai* and *Ye kaisa anyay data*. Unlike other studios, New Theatres did not exploit its talented artistes and Saigal did only one or two pictures a year. Another successful film from them was the Hindi version of *Doctor*, with Pankaj Mullick in the title role regaling the audience with popular songs like *Chale pawan ki chat* and *Guzar gaya wo zamana*.

The year 1941 was marked by several outstanding box-office hits from the Bombay region, including Wadia's epoch-making hit *Raj Nartaki*, starring renowned dancer Sadhana Bose, with music by Timir Baran and directed by Sadhana Bose's husband Modhu Bose in three languages, English, Hindi and Bengali. It was a landmark film, hailed as the first serious venture for the international market. Kidar Sharma's *Chitralekha*,

Saigal with Prithviraj Kapoor in *Dushman*

based on the story by the celebrated Hindi writer Bhagwati Charan Verma, with music by Ustad Jhande Khan, was widely acclaimed as a classic with a lyrical flavour. V. Shantaram had another hit, *Padosi*, a real masterpiece of cinematic art, highlighting the ideal of communal unity. Sohrab Modi brought out another historic spectacle *Sikandar*, starring Prithivraj Kapoor as Alexander, which turned out a big crowd puller with its grand sets and display of elephants and horses, along with powerful dialogues. But the most extraordinary film that created a virtual sensation in the country was Pancholi's *Khazanchi* from Lahore studios. A musical extravaganza, it was a trendsetter which popularized a mixture of light classical and folk music of Punjab by composer Ghulam Haidar, who later became a famous music director in Bombay. The film, an adaptation of *The Way of All Flesh* was an astounding success. So much so, that the Hollywood film of the novel was flashed as 'The English Khazanchi'. The film also introduced Lahore on the film map of India.

The onset of the war and the consequent rush of new investors in film production led to a galloping demand for star artistes, directors, scriptwriters and others connected with film production. This led to the disintegration of the old established studio system. New Theatres, which maintained their permanent unit of artistes, directors and other

Saigal with Uma Shashi and Nawab in *Chandidas*

technicians on a monthly salary basis could no longer sustain themselves and compete with their rivals who looked for quick and easy profits. The war also led to a marked increase in the population of cities and cinema halls were crowded with new movie-fans, largely rural industrial workers and troops who just wanted entertainment. The educated middle-class audience was outnumbered and new producers were no longer concerned about them. They only wanted star faces, dances and songs to ensure their profits. The 'all and sundry', with newly acquired wealth, hired stars and other well-known directors at fabulous fees and that is how the star system was born. New Theatres, with its liberal tradition and intellectual atmosphere, suddenly found itself isolated and the talented team which B.N. Sircar had so laboriously collected around him was compelled to migrate to Bombay which promised fame and fortune. The overall impact of these developments was a general lowering of the standard of films both in respect of their directorial values as well as their thematic ideas. The Indian film industry was now left without a formidable leader like New Theatres, which had provided the beacon-light to filmmakers all over the country. This was the natural outcome of the circumstances since it is inconceivable to think that any system could remain lasting in the fast-changing social and economic environment.

The disintegration of New Theatres began with the resignation in 1941 of Nitin Bose, one of their top directors and the creative genius behind Saigal's famous hits like *Chandidas* and *President*.

K.L. Saigal also migrated to Bombay the same year but returned to Calcutta in 1944 to complete *My Sister*, the last film he did for New Theatres. Directed by Hemchandra Chunder, with music by Pankaj Mullick, its success was mainly attributed to Saigal's captivating songs, like *Do naina matware, Chhupo na, oh pyari sajania* and the memorable hit *Ai qatib-e-taqdir mujhe itna bata de*. That New Theatres released a Saigal film after a three-year gap contributed to its immense popularity. The heroine's role was performed by the attractive Sumitra Devi who later joined the Bombay Talkies and appeared with Ashok Kumar in Bankimchandra's *Mashal*, directed by Nitin Bose.

My Sister portrays a brother's deep attachment for his sister for which he sacrifices his own desires and ambitions. For the first time, this film carried some scenes about the war, destruction by air raids and a blood-donation programme. Another notable feature of the film was that the composer Pankaj Mullick later re-recorded Saigal's songs in his own voice in 78 rpm records.

Devdas

Devdas is remembered as an all-time classic of Indian cinema, which immortalized New Theatres' P.C. Barua and K.L. Saigal. It was epoch-making, and marked the blossoming of Indian cinema; with its depiction of feelings and emotions it brought films closer to real life.

Based on renowned Bengali writer Saratchandra Chatterjee's popular novel which he wrote at the age of seventeen, *Devdas* was first filmed in 1928, in the silent period, by Naresh Mitra. P.C. Barua, a creative genius of his time, best remembered for directing *Devdas*, raised the level of his film to a solemn tragedy. He introduced a new style of acting, which was natural and unaffected, a departure from the current theatrical mode, and also adopted simple, easy-to-follow dialogues without any literary nuances. Barua played the title role in the Bengali version and K.L. Saigal in the Hindi one and both went on to become cult figures.

Devdas is the story of a young man, son of a feudal landlord, who has an abiding love for his childhood playmate Parbati, daughter of his poor neighbour of a lower status and caste. To prevent their growing attachment, Devdas is sent to Calcutta for university education and Parbati is married off to an aged widower. Devdas returns to the village but is helpless in stopping Parbati's marriage. Devdas goes back to the city, and drowns his sorrows in drink and the company of a singing girl Chandramukhi who gets attached to him. To serve and look after him, she even quits her profession but Devdas' condition deteriorates. On hearing about his miserable plight, Parbati comes to plead with him to stop drinking but in vain. Rather than follow her advice, he promises Parbati that he would come to see her before he dies. He has consumption, and his decline continues in spite of the devoted care and attention paid to him by Chandramukhi. In his fragile state of health,

Saigal in *Devdas*

and realizing that his end was fast approaching, he embarks on a journey to keep his promise. He travels all night to get to Parbati's village, only to die in front of her home. And Parbati, within the high walls of her home, hears that her Devdas is dead.

Barua's adaptation of the novel in *Devdas* reflected his own tragic view of a life starved of joy and laughter. His creative passion and technical innovations are revealed in his expert editing for dramatic

P.C. Barua

effect, close-up shots for image construction, and use of sound to suggest telepathic communication between the characters. Equally striking are the emotional patterns built through skilful handling of the visuals like conveying a sentiment or reaction through halting speech and using the intervening pauses during a dialogue for a more telling effect than the spoken word.

P.C. Barua, the intellectual prince from Gauripur, had learnt the art of filmmaking in France. He was not only the creator of *Devdas*, he was Devdas. Barua was a handsome young man, with aristocratic grace and charm, and had a deep voice which he used in a low, understated manner to enrich the content of visuals. Other features which distinguished Barua were his tragic and rather solemn intensity, his superb handling of actors, his instinct for detail and his subtle ways of depicting the characters' agony and anguish. For instance, his shooting of the train journey, portraying Devdas' intense suffering, with sounds from the rail track as the backdrop was indeed a marvel in cinematic art. Barua achieved great fame, popularity and adulation usually reserved for the stars. As the most eminent and successful creator of romantic-tragic drama, Barua received fabulous offers from Bombay producers to make *Devdas*-like films for them in Bombay. He rejected them, saying, 'It is not my field; it is a bazaar.' His fans' admiration for him could be judged from a letter addressed to him, published in a Calcutta paper, which said: 'We are inclined to include you in the category of the great thinkers of the present day. By producing the immortal *Devdas*, you opened a new way for the Indian film industry, and since then you are looked on as a great philosopher.'

Saigal with Jamuna Devi as Parbati in *Devdas*

Devdas can be seen as a film of social protest, against the evils of class and a caste-ridden society. There was some criticism for its highlighting the path of dejection, drink, disease and death, which could have an adverse influence on young minds. But people loved the hero Devdas; the film touched virtually a whole generation. The *Devdas* syndrome became synonymous with unrequited love. Barua's Hamlet-like personality and his premature death, like his Hindi-version-hero K.L. Saigal, through alcoholism, made him an icon of cinematic genius. Just before his death, he is reported to have said, 'Devdas was in me even before I was born, I created it every moment of my life, much before I put it on the screen, it was no more than a mirage, a play of light and shade, and sadder still, it ceased to exist after two hours. Now it's just a myth.'

The powerful appeal of the romantic-tragic hero made Devdas a cult figure. This set the pace for the popularity of the doomed hero on the Indian screen. The term 'Devdas' replaced the old 'Majnu', to symbolize a deeply dejected lover. For lovers, 'Devdasiat' became a fashion which implied a condition to be envied, cultivated and revelled in.

Both Bengali and Hindi versions of *Devdas* were released in 1935. Though K.L. Saigal was no match for Barua's attractive appearance and charm, he more than made it up with his enchanting melodies. The role of Parbati, the heroine, was played by Jamuna in both the Bengali and Hindi versions, while Chandramukhi was enacted by Chandrabati and Rajkumari respectively. Originally, Barua wanted Kananbala to play the part of Chandramukhi as she had already established her name and fame in Bengali cinema. But as she was bound by her contract with Madan Theatres, she could not accept Barua's offer. The phenomenal success of the film was also attributed to its marvellous music composed by Timir Baran (Hindi) and R.C. Boral and Pankaj Mullick (Bengali).

Apart from his sterling performance as Devdas, which made him Indian cinema's first superstar, Saigal also had a sensational walk-on part in the Bengali version as one of the visitors to Chandramukhi's *kotha* and sang two Bengali songs *Kahare je jodatey chai* and *Golap hoey uthuk phutey*. Saigal took pains to learn the meaning of each word of the songs and absorbed the mood and ambience of the scenes in which they were to be sung. Sung in a classical style in leisurely fashion, with pauses, the songs in Saigal's voice evoked unique beauty and serenity. Originally, Pankaj Mullick was scheduled to sing these songs but when he heard the recordings he felt he could not match the magical spell created by Saigal's

Saigal with Jamuna Devi in *Devdas*

voice. This was Saigal's Bengali debut and the New Theatres' controllers of production awaited the author Saratchandra Chatterjee's approval because they apprehended a negative public response to Saigal's imperfect Bengali accent. When Chatterjee arrived and heard the recording, he was greatly pleased and at once gave his approval by pointing out that non-Bengalis were not barred from visiting the salons of singing girls and

Saigal's rendition of the songs was justified in the scene. Later, Saigal acted in several Bengali films of New Theatres.

It was noted in some quarters that the tragic ending in *Devdas* did not conform to the Indian classical tradition in which there were only happy endings. In Sanskrit dramas there was no room for tragedy, since the Hindu mind treated life as a transitional state. But in the nineteenth century, Western influence had had its impact on Bengali literature and drama, and the element of a tragic ending had been already introduced before *Devdas*. Many literary stalwarts and critics consider the tragedy and its portrayal saturated with agony and anguish to be a far greater literary achievement than comedy. The emotional content of the tragedy has a powerful and enduring impact on the audiences and enlightens them about the intensity of human feelings and their meaning in life. All famous Indian love-legends—of Laila–Majnu, Heer–Ranjha, Sohni–Mahiwal and Mirza Sahiban—glorify true love with a tragic end and with the firm belief that the lovers would be united in the next life.

Compared with the Bengali version, the Hindi *Devdas*, which had a much larger reach all over the subcontinent, was a superhit. The dialogue and lyrics were written by Kidar Sharma, who created an amazing script, infusing its romantic-tragic plot with a revolutionary naturalness of tone. It was remarked, 'This isn't dialogue, this is the way we talk.' And that was precisely what Barua was looking for. And, of course, the greatest asset of the film was the golden voice of Saigal, who was already a celebrity with his recent remarkable success as a singer–actor in *Chandidas*.

Saigal was the first artiste to sing in a relaxed, natural and intimate style and his songs were essentially dialogue in the musical form. The camera work was done by Bimal Roy, a genius in his own right. The songs like *Balam aao baso mere man mein* were on everyone's lips throughout the country and Saigal became a household name and a virtual legend in his own lifetime. The movie itself brought name and fame to everyone, great or small, connected with New Theatres. Barua was proclaimed a frontrank filmmaker and New Theatres as the leading light of the Indian film industry. Never before had any film won such universal acclaim and achieved such astounding commercial success. It was hailed by the *Bombay Chronicle* as 'a brilliant contribution to the Indian film industry. One wonders as one sees it, when we shall have such another.'

Hearing Saigal sing *Dukh ke ab din bitat nahin*, sung in Desh raga in the thumri style, became an addiction for millions of Saigal fans. They

In *Devdas*

would throng to the cinema halls to watch Saigal, with his drooping lock of hair escaping from under the sola hat, carrying a gun and aimlessly wandering in the village outskirts on a hot afternoon looking for birds to shoot. I vividly recall my college days when boys would not only hum the songs but would memorize the dialogue and enjoy articulating it in friendly circles. For many fans, the most touching and memorable scene was Devdas lying in despair and singing, or rather whispering, in perfect cadence *Piya bin nahin avat chain* (sung in Raga Piloo), made famous by the great maestro Abdul Karim Khan. Spoken one word at a time, *Piya bin* connects into one piece and turns into a fantastic melody which has a mystifying impact on the listener. It is said that when Khan Sahib was told about this, he went to the cinema for the first time in his life and saw *Devdas*. Saigal's marvellous rendition of his thumri *Piya bin* brought tears to his eyes and Khan Sahib wept like a child. The other *Devdas* songs as sung by Saigal are still heard on the radio, but this one was never recorded on a disc and can be heard only by watching the film.

The Indian media has since used the word 'immortal' in relation to Barua, Saigal and the film *Devdas*. The film continues to be a reference point for Hindi melodrama and figures in the teaching of cinematography to film students.

In 1936, New Theatres produced the Tamil version of the film, which was equally successful, with Saigal singing two songs in Tamil. Later, two versions appeared in Telugu, the first by Vendantam Raghavaiah in 1953 and the second by Vijaynirmala in 1974.

Two decades after Barua's masterpiece, his distinguished cameraman Bimal Roy, who had come to Bombay and become a successful director and producer, came out with his remake of *Devdas* in Hindi (1955), starring the then-famous actor Dilip Kumar, with Suchitra Sen and Vijayantimala as Parbati and Chandramukhi respectively. Dedicated to Barua and Saigal, Roy presented his *Devdas* to the new generation who had neither seen the original version nor read Saratchandra's classic work. The older generation rated Barua's *Devdas* as far superior to Bimal Roy's. The ghost of *Devdas* has subsequently appeared in many Hindi films like *Mela*, *Babul*, *Pyasa* and *Kagaz ke Phool*.

After nearly fifty years, we have a new incarnation of *Devdas* in Sanjay Leela Bhansali's magnum opus. This fifty-crore-rupee extravaganza is the most expensive Indian film made so far, with its stunning sets, lavish decor and glittering costumes. Another version of *Devdas* planned by writer-director Gulzar in the 1970s, with Dharmendra, Hema Malini and Sharmila Tagore, did not materialize. But a group of senior citizens, who delight in praising the 1955 version with Dilip Kumar, dismiss the new *Devdas* as too dazzling for them.

Concert at Lahore

K.L. Saigal's visit in 1937 to Lahore, the cultural capital of north India, was indeed memorable. Saigal had by then achieved countrywide fame and his voice was heard in his films and in gramophone records. He was acclaimed as the greatest singer of India, and his fans included both the young and the old from every section of society. For music lovers of Lahore, to hear Saigal in person was an opportunity of a lifetime. As it happened, Saigal's public performance in Lahore was his first and last one there. His visit was advertised through newspapers and large posters that were put up at conspicuous sites all over the city, announcing his performance at Variety Theatre, set up at the All-India Exhibition, the largest of its kind ever to be held at Lahore's Minto Park, the plain outside Hazoori Bagh between the fort and the Ravi river. More than six decades later I still vividly recall the spell of Saigal's magic on the audience. I, then a teenager but an ardent fan, was in the audience too.

Lahore was historically famous for its accomplished performing artiste-dancers and singers who adorned the Mughal courts. The tradition continued during the Sikh rule. According to a contemporary account, Maharaja Ranjit Singh maintained a troupe of 150 dancing girls and musicians, who entertained the royal guests and dignitaries, including the visiting British Governor-General and his party. The institution of dancing girls continued to flourish during the British period. The sahibs used to attend nautch parties held by the Punjabi aristocracy. Every joyous occasion in Lahore was accompanied by entertainment with dance and music. Thanks to the patronage of the emerging rich business class, the landed gentry and the princely states in Punjab, the

Government College, Lahore

art of music and dance confined to the families of professional artistes for generations continued to thrive, thus keeping alive the traditional performing arts.

The historic entertainment quarters of Lahore, located in Hira Mandi, were the abode of accomplished, elegant and educated performing artistes, whose salons were the seat of culture visited by writers, poets and the rich. They had produced some of the most famous singers of India and provided artistes for the theatrical companies of Calcutta and Bombay and later for the film industry.

It was in Lahore in 1925 that the American pioneer of modern dance, Ted Shawn and his talented wife Ruth St Denis, were struck by the performance of leading Kathak dancer Pandit Hira Lal. A number of accomplished artistes from Lahore were invited by the princely courts, the chief patrons of performing arts in those days. It was the well-preserved tradition of classical music which inspired the great revivalist of Indian music, Pandit Vishnu Digambar Paluskar, to set up his first music teaching institution, Gandharva Mahavidyalaya, at Lahore in May 1901. The city was a leading centre of Urdu literature, with prestigious journals like *Humayun*, *Alamgir* and *Adab-e-Latif*. Along with the artistes, Lahore also had a knowledgeable audience. The most significant factor was the universal popularity of cinema, which brought together

A bazaar scene in Lahore, c. 1930

various sections of society—the elite, the intellectuals and the unlettered masses. The Punjabi affinity for cinema made Lahore the most attractive market for the film producers of Calcutta and Bombay.

Lahore was yet to emerge as an important centre of the film industry. The early ventures after the advent of talkies mostly failed at the box office. This had forced producers, directors, scriptwriters, actors and singers to seek their fortunes in Calcutta, then the leading centre of the

Indian film industry with prestigious companies like the Madan Theatres, New Theatres and the East India Film Company. The first successful Punjabi film *Sheila* was produced by K.D. Mehra in Calcutta and released all over Punjab in early 1937. Known for its lively people with a zest for enjoying life, Lahore was then called the 'Paris of the East'. It was a leading centre of education, with a chain of colleges and professional institutions, and the young student population of Lahore surpassed even those of the Presidency towns of Bombay and Calcutta.

After the advent of sound, a number of new cinema houses sprang up with the latest equipment and luxurious fittings. Before shows began, audiences in cinema halls would be entertained with music and popular gramophone records would be played, with Saigal topping the list. By 1937, in addition to his film songs, a number of non-film songs—ghazals and bhajans—also became equally popular and Saigal became a household name throughout the country. I recall how his famous bhajan *Suno suno hey Krishan kala* enthralled the women of Lahore. The city cinemas introduced weekly 'zenana' shows every Wednesday afternoon to which tonga-loads of women would come from all over the city.

By 1937, film music had struck roots in the domain of public entertainments. The possession of a gramophone and 78 rpm records of film songs became a status symbol. Saigal's records were so popular that they were continually played at gramophone shops and at some restaurants to attract customers. It was common to find crowds gathering to hear K.L. Saigal on the roadside in front of these spots. Youngsters would also be heard humming Saigal's hit songs like *Balam ayo baso more man mein* and *Ek bangla bane nyara*.

In those days, cinema was the chief source of music entertainment. The salons of accomplished singers, where clients were regaled, were accessible only to the affluent few. It was said that many singers would sing the ghazals of Urdu poets popularized by Saigal. Around this time, a few cinema houses in Lahore introduced a novel feature of combining a film show with a live song-dance performance. This was to attract the crowds by offering *'ek ticket mein do maze'* (two entertainments for the price of one). The films shown were often on their second run and the screening was interrupted three or four times for the live dance and song by a nautch girl.

Traditionally, Punjabis live with music, which dominates every facet of their lives from the cradle to the grave. No social or religious festivity is complete without song and dance. The old love legends of Punjab, such as Heer–Ranjha, Sassi–Punu, Sohni–Mahiwal and Mirza Sahiban are marvels of Punjabi poetry and an essential part of the folklore. The wandering minstrels of Punjab were legendary singers who popularized the fabled romances of the Land of Five Rivers. These immortal folk tales were narrated in a special style of singing, each with its individual composition intertwined with a particular raga, with its own haunting effect, which was loved and appreciated by all. The religious festivals and ceremonies were also celebrated with devotional music. Even hawkers selling their wares usually announced their presence in a musical fashion to attract customers. Then there were the plebeian poet-cum-singers who would recite satirical and humorous verses in popular film tunes and sell their leaflets of poems called *kissa*s for an anna a piece.

I vividly remember one hawker of such *kissa*s in Lahore who recited his poems in his melodious voice, regaling the audience of young and old who gathered around him.

One of the poems was as follows:

Sharam haya sade desh di,
Yaro sari udh gayi ai,
Rana ne purdab utaraya,
Mardan nu gairat na rahi ai.
Poncha khula howe salwar da,
Jinwain hathi kana nu marda,
Gal jumpar rang unabi da,
Salwar da latha chabi da.

(Friends, modesty has vanished from our land and we have become shameless. Women have discarded the purdah and menfolk have lost all sense of modesty. Women wear salwars with wide bottoms which wave like an elephant's ears. They wear purple-coloured shirts and their salwars are made of long cloth of an English 'key' brand).

Another satirical song sung by these street bards was:

Put pendu saab kahave,
Padhe wich kalej de.
Roti di than cake oh khave,
Ande biscuit cha udhave,

Wich kamiz de nala pave,
Te button pajame nu lave,
Padhe wich kalej de.

(A village boy studying in college is referred to as a *pendu* sahib. In place of *roti* (bread), he eats cakes, biscuits and eggs over cups of tea. He puts on a string (tie) in his shirt and holds his pyjama by buttons (instead of with a cord.)

Young women of the 1930s, influenced by the wave of social reforms, spread of education and exposure to modern trends, acquired a new lifestyle which marked the beginning of a new era. Some popular films like *Saubhagya Sundri*, starring Sulochana, and *Gun Sundri*, with Gauhar, glorified the Indian woman in the role of a wife. Music came to be patronized in middle-class homes and a number of schools sprang up in Lahore where young girls were taught to sing and play the harmonium. Soon, this came to be regarded as an additional qualification for marriageable girls.

Accomplished professional singers from the entertainment district of Lahore were now aspiring to become radio artistes and singing actresses in cinema. Lahore was famous for its traditional *gharana*s of classical musicians who imparted training to upcoming young artistes and groomed them to earn laurels in their profession. Lahore was emerging as the centre for recruiting budding stars: actresses, singers and dancers. Many of them rose to become leading figures in Bollywood and won countrywide fame.

This was the Lahore of the late 1930s, when Saigal performed there. Before the performance, large crowds gathered outside the booking windows at Variety Theatre. Youngsters hummed the ever-popular *Suno suno Krishan kala* and *Piye ja aur piye ja*. Tickets cost between twelve annas and seven rupees. I made a feeble attempt to get near a window to buy tickets in the rush but return empty-handed. My friend accompanying me then made an attempt, also without success. In the meantime, someone approached us with an offer to sell us two-rupee tickets for three rupees each. We grabbed the tickets and rushed into the hall. There was a makeshift stage set up in a tin shed. But for a few rows of chairs in the front, the seating was on flat wooden benches. The hall was packed to capacity, with a large number of people standing. Sitting on a bench in the centre of the hall, I watched as the audience was getting restless. They started whistling to attract the attention of the organizers. A tall person, wearing a black *achkan* and a sparkling white turban, jumped onto the stage. With folded hands he addressed the audience in a loud, clear voice, 'Brothers and sisters,' (although there were no 'sisters' in the hall) 'you are now going to see and hear the greatest singer of our time, K.L. Saigal who, as you all know, is our Punjabi brother and has come all the way from Calcutta to enchant us with his melodious voice. We are proud that he is without a parallel in India. Now, silence please, and let me go and bring our honoured guest to the stage.'

The tenor of homage and honour to Saigal was evident from the loud cries from outside: 'Kundan Lal Saigal *zindabad*, *gaane ka badshah zindabad*.' (Long live, Kundan Lal Saigal, the king of music).

Escorted by a team of organizers, Saigal, weighed down with garlands, walked up to the stage followed by someone carrying his personal harmonium which was his constant companion. Young-looking, with regular features, he was dressed in a tweed jacket and a polo-neck sweater, with a brown felt hat over his balding head. Taking off his hat and removing the garlands, his grey eyes lit up as he greeted the audience with his winning smile. There was an outburst of applause and shouts of 'K.L. Saigal *zindabad*'. Saigal took charge of his harmonium and pindrop silence prevailed as his regal voice rent the air with his famous song *Lag gai chat karejwa mein*. He followed it with *Andhe ki lathi tu hi hai, tu hi jiwan ujiara hat,* a popular song from *Dhoop Chhaon*. Scores of requests for other popular songs were made from the audience. Some of Saigal's fans stood up on chairs and benches. Pandemonium prevailed. Then someone ran up to the stage and shouted, 'Please stop making these requests, we should honour our worthy guest by requesting him to sing songs of his own choice.'

Now Saigal beamed at the audience and poured forth from the depth of his soul ghazals like *Ye tasruff Allah Allah tere maikhane main hat, Layi hyat aye kaza, Dil se teri nigah jigar tak utar gat*. There was a standing ovation after every song, followed by cries of 'once more'. Next came a favourite hit from *Pujarin*—*Piye ja aur piye ja, Akbat ki baten jane koi kya*.

Saigal concluded the programme with the soul-stirring melody: *Panchi kahe hot udas*. The audience was spellbound.

The show over, the crowds left the hall after a once-in-a-lifetime experience.

Ghazal King

Ghazal usne chheri, mujhe saaz dena,
Zara umr-e-rafta ko awaz dena.

(Someone has just stirred the muse of poetry, hand me an instrument to play. Let us recall the cherished days of our youth, passion and joy.)

This beautiful couplet highlights the deep and symbiotic relationship between poetry and music. In the Urdu tradition, the poet melds both these arts in the aesthetically appealing form of the 'ghazal', which he then uses as a vehicle to discover the meaning of life itself.

K.L Saigal, the incomparable 'ghazal king', owed his greatness to his extraordinary ability to identify with the spirit and mood of the poet and his poetry. He made a stupendous contribution to the popularization of Urdu poetry not only among the educated but also among the unlettered. There was something uncommon, even otherworldly, in his handling of the seven notes as they sparkled in his singing.

Saigal was an extraordinarily creative artiste, with mastery of both classical and light music. His fame and popularity as a singer of film songs and bhajans somewhat overshadowed his stunning performance as a ghazal singer. But the fact remains that he was the undisputed ghazal king. He preferred to sing ghazals at private gatherings and functions. And it was as a ghazal singer that he won the adoration of connoisseurs of music who seldom went to the cinema. They were enthralled by his matchless style of singing the verses of renowned poets of the nineteenth century. Saigal was also responsible in large measure for the revival of interest in the romantic Urdu poetry of the period and for popularizing the works of some eminent poets, such as Zauq, Seemab, Arzoo, Bedam, Hasrat Allahabadi and, of course, Mirza Ghalib.

The ghazal is the most popular form of Urdu poetry and with its romantic themes and flowery lyrics, it is most suitable to for musical rendering. It owes its origin to classical Arabic poetry but it flowered in Persian literature and became its most cultivated and important form of poetry when it came to India. The literal meaning of the word 'ghazal' is a tête-à-tête between the lover and the beloved. The Mughal period brought about a glorious fusion of Indian and Persian art and culture leading to the emergence of new musical forms, such as the thumri, dadra and the ghazal, all of which were suffused with amorous influences. In its pristine form, the ghazal represented the sublime love for the supreme creator but later, the bhakti content gave way to the worldlier and more realistic text based on passionate and emotional ties between man and woman. The poets called the divine love *ishq-e-haqiqi*, or true love, and passionate love *ishq-e-mejazi* or symbolic love.

The Persian ghazal dominated the Indian musical scene well until the beginning of the nineteenth century, before giving way to the Urdu ghazal, which followed the form, imagery and the theme of its precursor. While it deals with the whole spectrum of human existence, the principal emphasis is on unrequited love, mystical devotion, ridicule of orthodox customs and values and hypocrisy in thought and action, and the symbolic celebration of intoxication with wine to overcome the pangs of separation, longing and frustration.

Until the beginning of the twentieth century, the performing arts of dance and music were inseparable. If the song was the soul, dance represented the body. The courtesans or *tawaif*s of north India invariably embellished their ghazal singing with dance movements to express the emotions of love, jealousy, hope, despair and the passions, so familiar to lovers. Early English officials of the East India Company were charmed by the performance of native dancing girls as well as by their feminine beauty and graceful demeanour. A Persian ghazal by Hafiz, which finds mention in several contemporary accounts, was *Tazah ba tazah nu ban nu*, a beautiful melody in which the poet recommends doing everything with freshness, whether drinking, making friends or making love. Another popular ghazal by Hafiz was 'Song of Roshan', describing the heart-rending despair of the separated and the painful wait for the arrival of one's lover. When Persian gave way to Urdu, a language born through Indo-Persian contacts, the ghazal became the pride of Urdu poetry and has retained its pre-eminent position in Urdu literature and popularity with the people.

In its form, the ghazal is a collection of couplets, each of which is self-sufficient and a complete expression of an idea, feeling or thought. In a way, each couplet is a poem in itself. The verses portray the poet's thoughts and feelings based on his profound experience and understanding of love and life. Mystical verses abound in the works of nearly all Urdu poets. Wali Deccani, said to be the father of Urdu poetry and the master of the ghazal, has beautifully expressed the state of mind of the ghazal writer:

Shagal behtar hai ishqbazi ka
Kya haqiqi wa kya mejazi ka

(Love is the most desirable of all diversions
Be it earthly passionate love or spiritual.)

Before the ghazal appeared in the field of music, from the time of Amir Khusrau, poets would recite their verses tunefully and this practice still survives in *mushairas*, assemblies of poets. Classical vocalists rarely sang ghazals, preferring to offer the semi-classical forms of thumri and dadra. K.L. Saigal was one of the first eminent artistes to lend his melodious voice to the rendition of the ghazal. His perfect diction brought an array of rarefied emotions as he married music to poetry. Thanks to him, the ghazal became popular as a musical genre with lovers of music and people at large through his gramophone records.

Saigal was an ardent admirer of the accomplished, well-trained professional singing girls and was impressed with their style of singing thumris and ghazals. It is said that as a young boy in Jammu, he would sneak away to the house of a singing girl and listen to her practise. Later, he would try to emulate her. That was the only indication of his having received any kind of music training. A keen observer and a serious connoisseur of music would discover some flavour of the *kotha* style in Saigal's singing of light classical thumris and ghazals.

In *Karwan-e-Hayat*

Himself a poet, Saigal's creative genius provided a new form and content to the poet's verses by producing lifelike images to his words. He identified himself with the moods and feelings expressed by the poets and enthralled his listeners with his brilliant improvisations by stirring up similar emotions in them. He was well versed in Urdu literature and his cultivated love for Urdu poetry and sensitive disposition inspired him to portray the thought content of the verses in the most appropriate rhythmic and musical patterns. Saigal was himself a composer and practically all his non-film ghazals and songs were given a musical garb by him. Of all forms of music, it was the ghazal that appealed most to his creative genius as he sincerely shared the feeling and emotions expressed by the poet. He was a true and genuine interpreter of the lyrics of renowned poets like Zauq, Hasrat, Seemab, Ghalib and others.

In the words of the leading singing star of his days, the late Kanan Devi, 'The total quality of his singing was so understanding that it came to be hailed as Saigal's voice. His style of singing ghazals bears such a stamp of individuality that it is recognized all over India as the Saigal technique. Equally striking was his selection of ghazals for musical soirées and other functions, always appropriate to the atmosphere and environment.'

Saigal gave life to verses as he sang in his inimitable style, ghazals like *Matwalepane se jo ghata jhum padhi ha, chhati se dhuan utha hai jo bund padhi ha* by Arzoo. What an extraordinary rendering, that picturized a smouldering flame within the heart whose intensity was portrayed by the rising smokescreen of steam with a mere sprinkling of water on the chest! According to Pakistani scholar Hafiz Hazi Ahmad, Saigal was the first singer who sang the illustrious poet Iqbal's famous ghazal without distorting the pronunciation of *haqiqat-e-muntzir*:

> *Kabhi ai haqiqat-e-muntzir nazar aa libase-e-majaz mein*
> *Ke hazaron sajde tadap rehe hain meri jabin-e nyaz mein*

Before Saigal, ghazal singing was not very popular because there was the general impression that the singing would overshadow the meaning of the verses by distracting listeners to focus on the musical content. Saigal was the first artiste to dispel this notion by joining music to poetry. He actually succeeded in highlighting poetry's meaning with rhythm and melody, which embraced the ghazal's couplets. He played with words in a singular manner, never repeating a line in the same strain. He brought out the meaning of a verse as he felt it himself and then his majestic voice did all the rest to mesmerize the listeners. Saigal has applied his remarkable musical talents in ghazal singing as we observe in the following cases.

Lai hyat aaye kaza le chali chale
Apni khushi na aaye ham no apni khushi chale

Rahmat pe teri mere gunahon ko naz hai
Banda hun janta hun tu banda nawaz hai

Duniya mein hun duniya ka talabgar nahin hun
Bazar se guzra hun kharidar nahin hun

Shama ka jalna hai, ya sozishe parwana hai
Chand lafzon mein yahi ishq ka afsana hai

Many other singers have sung the same ghazals that Saigal decorated with his music but the magical effect on the listener's mind is lacking. A Pakistani scholar, Mushir Anwar Kamal Mustafa, paying tribute to Saigal in an Urdu magazine in 1959, points out that no ghazal singer before or after Saigal has ever been able to enthral the listeners with his prodigious style and divine voice along with the rare elements 'soz' and 'loch', words which defy translation into English—they are related to a state of mind, and associated with the soul or spirit. Saigal's expressions were spontaneous outpourings of feelings. His adaptation of the words followed the aesthetic principle of sound and sense and offered spiritual joy to the listeners. So much so that *paanwallas*, *tongawallas*, peons, clerks, hawkers, students and teachers could be heard humming Saigal's ghazals.

Pankaj Mullick, the renowned music director of his day, tells of his first meeting with K.L. Saigal in 1931 at the Calcutta radio station where he had arranged his first audition. Saigal sang an admirable ghazal for demonstration and displayed a certain excellence in playing the harmonium in accompaniment. Pankaj was so deeply impressed by his sense of melody and rhythm, his distinct pronunciation and neat articulation embellished with an exceedingly sweet and melodious tone, that it was broadcast the same night and Saigal was engaged as a regular artiste of the company.

So, it was as a ghazal singer that Saigal achieved his first recognition in the music world of Calcutta. This paved the way for his later selection as an artiste by New Theatres.

After emerging as the leading singer–actor of the film world, Saigal had little time for recording ghazals. In fact, after he moved to Bombay in 1941, he seems to have stopped singing ghazals for the Hindustan Records Company. At the same time, it should be noted that it was through his non-film songs that Saigal could be recognized primarily as a singer, followed by his supplementary role as an actor. Acting for him was a mere profession and a means to display his singing talents, whereas music was his life.

The mode and style of singing ghazals was Saigal's own innovation and his musical interpretation enhanced the meaning of the text. Saigal loved poetry and made it sound so significant and touching that listeners would understood the poetic works better by hearing his rendering, rather than by reading them. He himself set most ghazals to music. He sang these in classical ragas with sophistication and a sense of grace. Another notable point about his ghazal singing in private *mehfils* was that he was invariably in a relaxed and cheerful mood and would give a faint smile at a particularly poignant moment in the sad poetry.

We come across in his recordings, Bhairavis, Kafis, Bhimpalasis, Yamans, Piloos, Bageshwaris of every hue. He could move from one raga to another and produce a most exquisite blending of notes that delighted the listeners with their focus on the lyrical value of the ghazal. Another notable feature of his ghazal singing was the quality of the accompanying musical instruments. He kept at a distance the elaborate orchestra of those days that featured in his film songs. He was content with a tanpura, played softly enough to be just audible, his own harmonium and the tabla. While he considered the violin redundant, he did now and then use a sarangi as it followed his voice without any pretence.

For a full appreciation of ghazal singing the listener is expected to have some basic understanding of Indian classical music. It was in his ghazal singing that Saigal reached the pinnacle of his achievement as a singer. He had the rare ability to vary the pitch and volume of his voice easily to suit the requirement of the raga dominating the song and at the same time to inspire the listener to enjoy the beauty of the poet's creation.

In fact, to understand the musical genius of Saigal, it is imperative to listen to his ghazals again and again and experience the charm of his glorious voice and the intensity of his presentation as if the poet had written the verses especially for him.

Saigal sang only about thirty ghazals. Even after the issue of three LPs of Saigal's music in the 1960s, no ghazal records were available. HMV of Calcutta showed little interest in bringing out an LP disc of his ghazals until 1965 when I took up the matter with them and convinced their managing director Bhaskar Menon of the need to bring out two LPs of Saigal's ghazals and bhajans.

Saigal's Ghalib

Lovers of Urdu poetry are indeed indebted to Saigal for popularizing the Urdu ghazal, the pride of Urdu literature. The most celebrated poets like Mir, Dard, Ghalib, Zauq, Hasrat and Arzoo won the hearts of their readers through their poetry in the form of the ghazal. The acme of Saigal's artistic abilities was his rendition of Ghalib's ghazals. In fact, Saigal in his own way immortalized Ghalib by singing the master's choicest ghazals in his inimitable style. He sang the verses with a deep understanding of the poet's mind and the depth of his feelings and emotions. Saigal identified himself with the poet and seemed to live through the sorrows and joys as experienced and penned by Ghalib. Through his God-gifted voice, Saigal made the ghazal not just a melody but a soothing blend of thought and feeling. Many artistes have sung Ghalib, but none has been able to surpass Saigal, a fact that was acknowledged by the renowned Indian ghazal queen Begum Akhtar.

Mirza Ghalib is universally accepted as the greatest poet of the nineteenth century. Ghalib's philosophy of life, his unsentimental approach, adherence to a set of values and beliefs, and his capacity to enjoy life to the fullest and still remain aloof enabled him to treat every situation in his individual fashion with a humour that continues to enchant his readers even today. Saigal was an avid reader of Urdu literature, and Ghalib's philosophy seemed to have had a great impact on him. This is evident from contemporary accounts of Saigal's lifestyle and his lack of interest in material wealth and even in his own professional success, fame and popularity.

Saigal had a free and independent mind and followed his instincts to nurture his creative genius. Music was a passion with him; it was

A scene from *Omar Khayyam*

his life and the voice of his soul. A keen and sensitive observer of life and man's relationship with God, Ghalib expressed his thoughts and feelings in his poetry. Both Saigal and Ghalib were like sufi saints and in their creative art they found the most effective instrument for sublime communion with the Ultimate. Ghalib was a remarkable man, free of any kind of religious zeal, a strange combination of a transcendental genius, a mystic and a bohemian. Along with his personal experience of the vicissitudes of life, he was endowed with a deep insight into human nature. He created a fresh vocabulary to adorn the form and content of his poetry. But whereas Ghalib, the greatest Urdu poet of all time, was conscious and confident about his greatness, Saigal was full of humility and had little consciousness of his own pre-eminence as an artiste.

Saigal's devotion to the bottle and a detachment from his own life and environment could be attributed to Ghalib's influence on him. Neither ever lost his balance or indulged in unbecoming behaviour. Both were gentlemen to the core and drank to stimulate their creative genius. Saigal seems to echo the thoughts and feelings of Ghalib as expressed in his couplet:

Maiy se garz nishat hai kis rooh-siah ko
Ik guna bekhudi mujhe din raat chahiye

(Who is the accursed one who seeks pleasure and happiness from wine?
I merely seek to remain in a state of stupor day and night.)

Then we have Saigal singing Ghalib's appeal to the *saqi* not to deny
him wine.

Piha de oak se saqi jo mujh se nafrat hai
Pyala gar nahin deta na de sharab to de

(If you despise me oh *saqi*, do not give me the cup if you so desire. But
do not deny me the wine; just pour it into my cupped hands)

In his well-researched book on Saigal's music, eminent scholar and
musicologist Raghava Menon describes several incidents in Saigal's early
life. In Moradabad, during Saigal's itinerant years, a sarangi player,
Imtiaz Ahmad, first noticed the young Saigal's singing talent as he sang
Abdul Karim Khan's thumri on a deserted railway platform. Imtiaz took
him home and asked him to sing whatever he pleased while he carefully
tuned his sarangi. Then Saigal sang a Ghalib ghazal, *Dayam pada hua
tere dar par nahin hun main*, almost whispering, his lips hardly moving,
and tailoring the volume of his voice to the small room in which they
sat. This is the first inknown instance of Saigal singing specially before
an outsider.

Even with his knowledge of Urdu poetry Saigal chose to sing only
Ghalib, testifying to his deep fondness for the poet. It is not surprising
that of all the ghazals sung for recording, Saigal gave the highest
preference to Ghalib. Pankaj Mullick has also mentioned that Saigal
selected an admirable ghazal for his audition test at Calcutta radio
station and this was presumably also a Ghalib number.

Saigal was the first artiste to sing Ghalib in a way that appealed to the
masses, thus contributing towards the poet's fame and popularity even
with people not well versed in Urdu. The first Ghalib ghazal recorded by
Saigal was *Nukta chin hai gham-e-dil usko sunaye na bane* in *Yahoodi
ki Ladki* in 1933. It became an instant hit. Listeners were enthralled by

the concluding couplet as sung by Saigal—*Ishq par zor nahin hai ye woh atish Ghalib, ke lagai na lage aur bujhai na bane.*

Among other Ghalib ghazals popularized by Saigal were: *Main uneh chhedun aur kuchh na kahe, Har aik baat pe kahte ho tum ki tu kya hai, Ishq mujhko nahin wahshat hi sahi* and *Wo aake khwab mein.* Ghalib's masterpiece, which Saigal sang so poignantly that he virtually created a visual image of a dejected lover in utter despair probing his way out of his deep sorrows, runs as follows:

Aah ko chaahiye ek umar asar hone tak
Kaun jita hai teri zulf ke sar hone tak
Gham-e-hasti ka asad kis se ho juz marg-e-ilaj
Shama har rang mein jalti hai sahar hone tak

(It takes a lifetime for a sigh to be effective. But who lives long enough to win your tresses. Death is the only ultimate cure for the sorrows and sufferings of existence. The candle burns anyhow until the dawn, in different shades and colours).

Saigal's choice of Ghalib's poetry was most striking and it was this selection which was taken up in *Mirza Ghalib,* produced in 1954 by Sohrab Modi and starring the singer–actress Suraiya, Saigal's heroine in the 1945–46 films *Tadbir, Omar Khayyam* and *Parwana.*

Though film music brought Saigal fame and popularity, he preferred to sing his favourite self-composed ghazals and Ghalib's verses at private informal gatherings. There is an amusing episode recounted by Saigal's cousin Chaman Puri about an exclusive party thrown by the maharaja of Burdwan where champagne flowed from a special bottle with a gold tap. The guests kept asking Saigal to sing *Balam ayo baso more man mein.* The maestro would not break his own rule but he did not want to displease the gathering either. So he simply repeated the line twenty times till the guests laughed out their persistent request.

It has been remarked by some music critics that Saigal was not very proficient in the higher octaves, preferring to sing in a lower pitch. This is, however, not true. Saigal could pitch his voice with ease and enthral his listeners. In fact, it is necessary to listen to Saigal's rendition of Ghalib's ghazals, universally appreciated for their lyrical and literary quality, in order to grasp the sweep and range of his melodious voice. It

In *Karwan-e-Hayat*

is indeed amazing to find how Saigal so wonderfully identified himself with the spirit and mood of Ghalib as he sang verses recounting different aspects of life.

Saigal popularized an often elusive and philosophic poet like Ghalib by highlighting the depth and beauty of his verses. Ghalib, with his distinctive style, always presented the chief characters of the ghazal in a new light—the lover, his beloved, his rivals and others responsible for the separation of the lovers. When dealing with the Creator, and man's relation with Him, Ghalib treats the subject unsentimentally and with detachment, upholding his personal beliefs and self-esteem as illustrated in the following couplet:

Bandgi mein bhi wo azad-o-khudbin hain ke hum
Ulte phir aye dar-e-kaba agar va na hua

(I bow to you but my self-respect dictates to me that I will turn my back immediately if I find the Kaba door closed.)

Mirza Ghalib

Saigal employed his musical genius to emphasize not the literal meaning of the poetry but its deeper interpretation. He manipulated his voice to play a subordinate role to his music and give prominence to the text of poetry sung by him. Ghalib seemed to materialize in person in Saigal's rendition of his verses with love and devotion. According to Raghava Menon, Saigal's music had freshness and inspiration. Each ghazal was composed across the whole scale, bringing into focus the key sections of the raga's scale, and the phrasing changed from song to song.

What a superb affiliation—a musical genius and a poetic wizard! The Saigal–Ghalib duo has bequeathed to us a phenomenal treasure of melodies which will haunt music lovers for generations.

The Singer as a Poet

The dawn of the twentieth century saw a revival of Indian performing arts, notably the classical music tradition that had survived through the ages. It was the dedicated zeal of visionaries like Vishnu Digambar Paluskar and Vishnu Narayan Bhatkhande who worked hard to popularize Hindustani music through the medium of public concerts and music teaching centres. The first teaching institution, the Gandharva Mahavidyalaya, was set up at Lahore in May 1901.

When Saigal was growing up, few thought of music as a career. However, from his early childhood, Saigal had come under the influence of itinerant singers and mendicants and also learnt to sing bhajans from his mother Kesar Devi, who encouraged his interest in devotional music. As a young lad Saigal took an active part in the Ram Lila celebrations at Jammu and he usually played the role of Sita, a singing heroine. As a school boy, he would attend *kirtan*s in temples and showed an astonishing understanding of music. His formative years were greatly influenced by his association with Sufi Salaman Yusuf, a Muslim dervish at whose *dera* music was a daily activity. Here Saigal practised his singing and held discussions with other musicians, some of whom were poets as well. An avid reader of Urdu literature, Saigal learnt to express his thoughts and ideas in verses.

It is a little-known fact that Saigal was a poet and is said to have recited his verses at private gatherings. No recordings are, however, available except the extraordinary devotional song written and composed by him, *Main baithi thi phulwari mein, ek sakhi aa gayi aur boli,* which was issued by the Hindustan Records of Calcutta in 1945. It is a remarkable devotional piece which reveals the spiritual side of his personality and his Sufiana approach to the philosophy of life. According to Chaman Puri, Saigal was a great devotee of Lord Krishna and often sang bhajans with his mother. He believed that God is within us and without us and we are only sparks of the Divine. He speaks about a devotee of Lord Krishna who is wandering in search of the Lord until an inner voice bids her to close her eyes and awaken the inner vision to see and realize His presence.

Tab man ne mithi baat kahi
Kyon tune itni baat gahi
Ghar baithe pee pa sakati thi
Main bidhi bataun wo kya thi
Bahar ke naina moond sakhi
Aur nain hriday ke khol sakhi
Ab apne munh se bol sakhi
Sakhi kaun des raje piyra.

There is an authentic account of Saigal writing this bhajan while lying with his head in the lap of his wife Asharani and restlessly looking for the most appropriate words to express his thoughts. As the full song could not be covered in the ordinary 78 rpm record, a special, larger twelve-inch record was brought out. The reverse also carried Saigal's song *Hamjoliyon ki thi toliyaan, vo kar rahin thi thatoliyaan. Kuchh mast thi sangeet mein, kuchh khelti thi holiyan.* This is easily one of his finest compositions, full of shringar rasa, in which Saigal describes the frolic and love play of young maidens with their consorts on their honeymoon night as witnessed by a dejected woman pining for her mate. Saigal continued with his attachment to devotional music even after attaining stardom.

His maiden film success was in the New Theatres' *Puran Bhakt* where he sang four bhajans, all of which became hits and contributed to turning the film into a box-office hit even in the non-Hindi speaking parts of the country. Now, after over sixty years, music lovers still enjoy ever-popular bhajans like *Bhajun main to bhav se Siri Girdhari* and *Radhey Rani dey daro na bansuri mori.* His very first recording, *Jhulana jhulavo,* in classical form, with a hori *Hori re Brij rajdulare* on the reverse released as a 78 rpm in 1932–33 created a sensation. By now, many middle-class homes had acquired gramophones. I recall a group of people standing outside the gramophone shop in Anarkali, Lahore, listening avidly to this record. Even today, this melody continues to delight fans of Saigal, spanning three generations.

After the success of *Puran Bhakt*, the bhajan *Andhey ki lathi, tu hi hai, tu hi jeewan ujiara hai,* in *Dhoop Chhaon* (1935) brought him still greater fame, but it was in 1937 that Saigal recorded one of his all-time greats, *Suno suno hey Krishan kala,* which brought in womenfolk amongst his horde of fans. It is said that this famous bhajan came from Saigal's pen. Saigal was now a household name and listeners felt the sentiments of a great devotee in his voice and his articulation of the pious wording.

Most Hindu religious music is associated one way or another with the bhakti tradition, which came to occupy a central role in Hindu culture around the twelfth century onwards. Music, playing a central role in bhakti culture, is considered a form of worship, a means of direct communication with and ultimate union with God. Followers of Chaitanya Mahaprabhu and Sant Tulsidas concentrate on singing bhakti *geet* (devotional songs). India's variety of devotional music played an important role in the cultural life of the people without any distinction whatsoever of class, caste or creed.

In *Shah Jehan*

Saigal with Kanan Bala in *Lagan*

In *Dharti Mata* (1938), Saigal sang the soothing, devotional melody *Kisne ye sab khel rachaya, Kisne ye sab saz sajaya*, in which he pays his homage to the Creator. Saigal reaches the pinnacle of his glory as the lead in *Bhakt Surdas* (1942). He brings the saintly character to life by identifying completely with the saint and his complete dedication to Lord Krishna. The bhajans in the film, *Kadam chale aage, man pachhe bhage* and *Nayan heen ko rah dikha prabhu* were great hits, along with a very lively duet with Raj Kumari—*Sar pe kadam ki chhaiyan, muraliya baj rahi*. Interestingly, Saigal played the role of a poet in three other films, *Chandidas*, *Lagan* and *Shah Jehan*.

Untouched by his own achievement, Saigal kept away from publicity. His wife and other family members were cognizant of his poetic genius, but he never dwelt on it. Creative people receive inspiration from the invisible or the cosmos and, as Ghalib put it:

> *Aaten hain gaib se ze mazamin khyal mein,*
> *Ghalib sarire khama nawai sarosh hai.*

(These thoughts emanate from the heavens, O Ghalib; your pen is merely a scribe of the voice of the gods).

There is a lyric written by Saigal in his handwriting in Urdu on his personal letterhead, a copy of which was given to me a few years ago by Saigal's daughter, the late Bina Chopra. It is interesting to observe Saigal's monogram KLS on his letterhead with the message 'God is Love' inscribed below. Apparently, Saigal, like many of his generation, was greatly influenced by the teachings of Swami Vivekanand on Vedanta philosophy. Vedantists express the truth of God, Brahman, as *Sat-chit-ananda*, indicating that God is Existence, Consciousness and Love itself.

Given below are the lyrics that describe pangs of separation when the loved one is far away. This poetic expression of *Pardes mein rahne wale aa* suggests a personal experience of Saigal himself.

> *Ab dil ko nahin hai chain zara*
> *Pardes mein rahne wale aa*
> *Hai zabt ki had se dard sawa*
> *Tariq padhi dil ki duniya—*
> *phir apni mohni shakal dikha*
> *Phir pyar ki batain ake sunah!*
> *Pardes mein rahne wale aa.*

Jab subah ke rangin jalwon mein
Mastana hawa lehrati hai
Phulon ko apne dard bhare
Jab bulbul geet sunati hai—
Ek sanp sa dil par loteta hai
Jab yaad kisi ki aati hai—
Pardes mein rahne wale aa.

Pardes mein ja kar tu goah
Ulfat ki ghatain bhul gaya—
Ankhon se ojhal hote hi,
Wo pyar ki batain bhul gaya
Khilwat ke jalwon ki duniya,
Khilwat ki raten bhul gaya
Pardes mein rahne wale aa.

Raton ko kisi ki furkat mein
Uth uth ke ansoo roti hun
Barsat ki kali raton mein
Bistar pe akeli soti hun
Aur dil ko daba kar hathon mein
Nakam tamana hoti hun
Pardes mein rahne wale aa.

Madhosh massarat ho ho kar
Har shakh shajar par jhumati hai
Kis zauk se bulbul aa aa kar
Phulon ki mahak ko chumati hai
In meri dono ankhon mein
Andher ze duniya ghumati hai
Pardes mein rahne wale aa.

Ambava ki unchi dalion par
koylia shor machati hai
Pi pi jo papiha karta hai

tabahi dil par ho jati hai
Bulbul ke tara non se dil par
ik hairat si chha jati hai
Pardes mein rahne wale aa.

In hijar ke lambe wakfon ka
tujh ko koi ahsas nahin
Barsat ka mausam beet chala
milne ki abhi tak aas nahin
kya lutf hai aise jeene mein
piytam jab apne paas nahin
Pardes mein rahne wale aa.

Tu aye to tere charnon mein
main apna sis nava dungi
is dukhiya dil ki bipta ka
kuchh tujh ko haal suna dungi
jo dag alam hain seene mein
ek ek tujhe dikhla dungi
Pardes main rahne wale aa.

(I am feeling completely restless
Come back from your distant abode!
Unable to control any more, my pangs
of separation have only multiplied and despair
has enveloped my being.
Now again, show me your charming
face and talk of love and romance
Come back . . .

When in the colourful glory of dawn, that
enchanting breeze blows—
And the nightingale chants those heart-rending
melodies to the flowers—
I am overwhelmed with grief as I pine for you
Come back . . .

It seems after going to your distant
abode, you have forgotten all promises of love—
out of sight, out of mind, you
do not even remember those romantic exchanges.
Also vanished from your thoughts are those lonely
nights and the despairing world of the afflicted ones.
Come back . . .

Pining in separation of my loved one
I wake up repeatedly to shed tears
During the dark rainy nights
all by myself I lie down on the bed to sleep
And holding my heart in my palms
I suffer with unfulfilled desire
Come back . . .

Intoxicated with joy
every branch of a tree is dancing
And how fondly the nightingale
comes to relish the fragrance of flowers
But I am surrounded only by despair and darkness
Come back . . .

The nightingale is cooing loudly
On the tall branches of the mango tree
And the chirpings of the sparrow
destroy my peace of mind
And the nightingale's chants
create a sensation for my heart
Come back . . .

You have no idea of this long period of separation.
The rainy season is nearing its end but there
is still no hope of our getting together,
What fun is there in living when the loved
one is not with you,
Come back . . .

When you come, I will bow my head at your feet. I will
relate to you the anguish and pain of my heart. Also, I will
show you all the scars of my heart caused by this separation.
Come back from your . . .)

These lyrics, penned by Saigal, are in the voice of the *nayika*, or
young heroine, pining for her hero.

In his poem *Main baithi thi phulwari mein* Saigal elevates earthly
love into a spiritual one when he points to the '*sundar chabbi*' or the
'dazzling aura' of Lord Krishna.

That Saigal was spiritually inclined and involved in mysticism is
endorsed by his late son Madan Mohan, in a press interview in 1973. He
says that a few months before his death, Saigal would sit in the balcony
with his harmonium early in the morning and sing his favourite bhajans.
There is also one devotional song which Saigal composed with great
thought and feeling in the last days of his life. He had it recorded privately
and brought the master disc home. It was entitled *Hari bina koi kam na
aayo*. It was never released in the market. It ran as follows:

> *Hari bina koi kam na aayo*
> *Is jhoothi maya ke karan*
> *heera janam ganvayo . . . .*
>
> *Maya sagi na man saga*
> *Saga na ye sansar*
> *Lal das is jiva ka*
> *Sada visarjan har*
> *Istri kahe main sang chatungi*
> *Khos khos dhan khayo*
> *Chalti ber mod mukh baithi*
> *Palak na der lagayo*
> *Sab sneh hi sneh karat hain*
> *Inhi ke hath bikayo*
> *Chhut gaya jab kanth se dora*
> *Rat mil phunk jalayo.*

(The only saviour is Hari, the Lord. We are wasting this invaluable life in
pursuit of deceptive materialism. There is no true or real attachment in

Saigal in *Chandidas*

this transient world. The wife shares your material wealth and promises to depart with you. But when the end comes, she also turns her face away. I am sold to these attachments and when I breathe my last, they will get together to light the funeral pyre and turn me into ashes).

Saigal wrote and sang these words only for his family. The depth and intensity of his feelings and his realization of the transience of human existence is expressed beautifully in simple words.

Some of the phenomenal impact of Saigal's singing is also attributed to the poetic genius in him, which produced the perfect words clothed in most appropriate notes, giving life to the music and poetry. Listeners would be overwhelmed with tears of joy induced by the *rasa* or delight created by the melody. Eminent music director Pankaj Mullick, who was extremely fond of Saigal, mentions that the tonal quality of Saigal's songs with his wonderful command over the three octaves and special capacity for maintaining unvarying pitch was so outstanding that it earned the epithet of 'Saigal's voice'.

According to a graphic account attributed to his wife Asharani, Saigal received astounding applause when he sang at a music conference held at the Allahabad University Senate Hall in 1935. Eminent maestros of music of the time present there included Ustad Faiyaz Khan, Pandit Onkarnath Thakur, V.D. Paluskar, Narayan Rao Vyas and Vinayak Rao Patwardhan. Saigal sang his popular film-hits from *Chandidas*, *Devdas*, *Yahoodi ki Ladki* and *Karwan-e-Hayat*, followed by some bhajans and ghazals. Young students continuously requested for 'once more Saigal', with loud clapping. Saigal came down from the stage and lifted up his mother, a frail old woman who was in the audience watching the show, and said, 'Listen, Mother, listen, they are shouting for me to sing. They don't want me to stop. They think that I am a musician.' Describing this incident, Raghava Menon adds, 'To his mother the enormous audience rising to its feet to hear the golden voice of her son must have been the fulfilment of a dream. After what had seemed to her a lifetime, her son had been recognized. It must have been a touching scene.'

Another notable artiste of his days, Pahari Sanyal describes a special *jalsa* arranged by him at Calcutta (1938) in honour of Faiyaz Khan, referred to as Aftaab-i-Maussiqi (the sun in the world of music), the greatest classical singer of his time, where Saigal regaled the great maestro for hours. About Saigal's performance Faiyaz Khan said, 'We have been singing for generations in the family but we could never dream of singing like this, in the sense that he is such an effortless singer.' Faiyaz Khan then wanted to initiate Saigal as his disciple, an offer to which Saigal gladly responded. Then followed the ceremony of '*Ganda bandhan*'. There is another anecdote which mentions that when Faiyaz Khan first heard Saigal's *Jhulana jhulavo*, in Asavari Gandhari, he himself sang it in the same raga but conceded that he could not match Saigal's enchanting rendition of the song. He reportedly told Saigal that he did not need to learn anything from anyone else. This one song established Saigal's deep classical mastery because he even made the innovation of doing the *alaap* in pure Asavari and singing in Gandhari, a departure from the general rule of adopting the same ragini for both the *alaap* and melody.

Saigal was a versatile artiste who could achieve total oneness with the spirit of music. He sang impeccably in different styles and forms as well as in several languages—Bengali, Punjabi, Tamil, Hindi, Urdu and Persian. A music lover is enthralled by Saigal's diction and articulation of words like *'Diwana hun'*, or a whole phrase like *'Apna aap chhupaya'*, and he can easily discern a *komal gandhar* in a hori, in Kafi that highlights its glittering purity. In some songs, the use of a raga or the mere musical ingenuity of a composition would delight the listener. Then there is a strange enchanting mixture of speech and song in marvellous compositions like *Piye ja, aur piye ja* and *Ek raje ka beta lekar.*

During the 1930s and 1940s, there were hardly any magazines or journals which would publish interviews with performing artistes. There is, however, one interview of Saigal by Kirit Ghosh, editor of a Bengali magazine *Jayathi*. Ghosh was a product of Shantiniketan and took a keen interest in the arts and in music. To one of Kirit Ghosh's questions, Saigal answered, 'I am not a singer, not really. I can only be called a phraser. I have had no true classical training except what I have heard and remembered. I know very little of the real thing. I do not think of a song in terms of its notes, at least not exclusively. This is not even true when I am learning it or playing it on the harmonium when I sing it. I think of the meaning of the words and wrap the tune around the words. I have no clear understanding of the grammar of music. I manage to sing because of a strong feeling about how certain sounds should feel in a given raga. I have a certain feeling about how the *dhaivat* should feel in Malkaus, and the *madhyama* and also the nature of the *nishad*, in its relationship with the *shadja*. This changes from raga to raga. I do not know whether this feeling is right to have for I have never been taught Malkaus by a musician. It is the same with Asavari, which has a curious *madhyama* or the magical relationship between the *gandhara* and the *dhaivat* in Bhairavi and the strange urge to bring in an occasional *teevra madhyama* into it.'

To another question he answered, 'My favourite raga is Bhairavi. To know Bhairavi is to know all the ragas. You know how it is. There is Todi in it, there is Kafi in it, and Bhimpalasi and Bhairavi and the flavour and scent of so many ragas. In fact with any three notes of Bhairavi you can have a *dhun* and the possibility of another song. If I had Bhairavi I would not pine for any other raga very much.'

At another point in the interview, Saigal observed, 'People who learn to sing with the help of their ears alone cannot explain how they do it. All I can say about my own singing is that I do not use ten notes if I can manage to do the same with one. I have to make one note, and do the work which a trained singer does with ten. This is because I know very little.'

Saigal was also the first non-Bengali to be permitted and blessed by Gurudev Tagore to sing Rabindra Sangeet.

Saigal and the
Kotha Culture

As a young boy in Jammu, Saigal is said to have been influenced by professional singing girls. He used to hear them practising in their *kotha*s under the supervision of their ustads. The *kotha*s were still alive during Saigal's time and the traditional performing arts of dance and music were being preserved by this professional class referred to as *baiji*s. They entertained the music lovers at their salons and were invited on festive occasions by the aristocracy for private *mehfil*s. They usually presented semi-classical Hindustani music—thumri, dadra and ghazal—and sang the lyrics in a deliberate style which showed evidence of thorough classical training.

It is unfortunate that these talented professional artistes and singers were marginalized in society. The pursuit of music in middle-class homes was taboo, but after the advent of recording, the gramophone company had to depend upon these professional singers to sustain their business. Well-known male exponents of classical music declined to be recorded as they were reluctant to share their knowledge of music and become accessible to the public. The *baiji*s on the other hand readily agreed to be recorded and their discs earned large profits. This encouraged the Gramophone Company of Calcutta to set up their recording studios in Lahore, Bombay and Madras. In the process, *baiji*s also gained some respectability as gramophone singers. Among these are many who are still remembered even after a lapse of over eight decades for their melodious voices and enchanting style of presentation. Lovers of music speak nostalgically of the records of Gauhar Jan of Calcutta, Zohra Bai Agrewali and Malika Jan. Zohra Bai said to have perfected the art of compressing a raga to

Gauhar Jan of Calcutta

three and a half minutes, which was later appreciated and adopted by
maestros like Abdul Karim Khan and Fayaz Khan.

During his peripatetic days, K.L. Saigal seems to have visited the
*kotha*s of professional singing girls and was found to have been familiar
with the manners and customs followed at these venues. On his part,
Saigal would have imbibed the peculiar characteristics and style of their
art of singing. The special flavour of the *kotha* style is discernible in
Saigal's *Lakh sahi han peeki batiyan—ek sahi na jaye*, in *Rahmat pe
teri mere gunahon ko naz hai* and in *Aah ko chahiye ek umar asar hone
taq*. According to Raghava Menon, 'Saigal is an immortal example of
the culture of the *kotha*. It is extremely difficult for any artiste to sing
in the *kotha* style since it requires a rigorous discipline and restraint
along with musical know-how and classical training.'

There is a graphic account by Saigal's friend, G.N. Joshi, a distinguished
musician, in his book *Down Melody Lane* about their visit to a *kotha* at
Allahabad. Both had gone there to participate in a music conference in
1935. Their host, a local zamindar and a patron of musicians, took them
to the salon of a leading singing girl of the city. Joshi writes:

During dinner, someone suggested that we should go and have a taste of the gay musical night-life of the city. The young zamindar was, of course, familiar with the most reputed joints, and so off we all drove. In those days, in decent society, music was taboo—it was considered immoral to learn or listen to music—much more so for girls. I had heard a lot about the '*mujra mehfil*' (song and dance performances at the client's request) of the dancing girls and my curiosity was aroused; I was soon slowly following the other three up the steps of the singing girls' house.

At the entrance we were greeted by a middle-aged lady with a broad smile and the traditional salutation '*Adabaraz*'. We walked into an elegantly furnished chamber, brilliantly lit. The entire floor was covered with soft, richly coloured woollen carpets and mattresses.

Moments later two young girls, just out of their teens, entered from a side room. Having seen the film *Devdas*, they found Saigal's presence in person both awe-inspiring and highly pleasing. Saigal's friendly approach and unassuming manner soon dispelled their awe. An exuberant and intelligent conversation ensued. It was full of witty and spontaneous repartee in which these girls are specially trained, and with which Saigal appeared to be quite familiar. For me, this was a new and revealing experience, and I watched the scene with interest. One of the girls approached us with a tray of '*paanpatti*s' and when my turn came, I was so confused and nervous that the girl gave a mischievous smile as my trembling fingers lifted the *paan*. I muttered my thanks, '*Shukriya*', and pocketed the offering. I dared not eat it.

Of the two young girls, one was an accomplished singer with a rich, sonorous voice, and the other was an expert dancer. Thumri, the most captivating style in Hindustani music, has its home in UP. The Banarasi or Purab form of presenting it has no parallel in light classical music. The dancer used her feet, hands, fingers, neck, eyes and eyebrows most expressievely to illustrate the song. After another item—a Kathak dance—Saigal and the zamindar paid the girls and we rose to go.

It was about 2.30 a.m. when we got back to the zamindar's *kothee*. It was situated on the river bank, not far from the confluence of the Ganga and Jamuna. Cool breeze brought fragrance from the garden below, while the full moon turned the river milky white. Saigal was in a happy mood and started humming. The zamindar produced a harmonium which I started playing. Saigal requested me to join him in singing.

Taking the cue from the notes he hummed, I began a thumri in Mishra Khamaj—*Mane nahee samiya*. Instantly, Saigal took up the refrain and then there followed a musical duet. Saigal then started *Babul mora*, his *piece de resistance* in Bhairavi. The first rays of the sun heralding the dawn brought us down to earth.

From times immemorial, the Indian woman performing artiste has been an integral part of society. Referred to with different appellations, including *ganika*, *kanchani*, *nautch girl*, *tawaif*, and *baiji*, she has preserved our traditional performing arts of classical music and dance. In recent past, the great Urdu poets like Mir, Momina and Ghalib portrayed her as larger than life. Some singing girls earned name and fame and became celebrities of the music world.

Some artistes from Saigal's time, who transitioned from the *kotha* to the studio and stage and whose melodies continue to haunt the old generation of music lovers, were as follows:

Janki Bai of Allahabad (1880–1934)

Born in Banaras, Janki Bai and her mother were deserted by her father. They went to Allahabad and joined the team of a rich *kotha*

singer. Janki Bai had intensive music training from the famous Ustad Hassu Khan of Lucknow. Her nickname, Chhapanchhuri, is attributed to the fifty-six knife scars she got from a jealous suitor. A very accomplished artiste, she was also a poet; her *Diwan-e-Janki* was published around 1920. In 1911 she even gave her performance along with the legendary Gauhar Jan of Calcutta in the presence of Emperor George V and received a reward of 100 guineas. HMV recorded over

Janki Bai Chhapanchhuri of Allahabad

250 songs on 78 rpm discs during 1910–30. According to one report, there would be traffic snarls when her records were played at shops in Allahabad. She contributed in no small way to the spurt in gramophone sales. Several of her records registered print orders of more than 25,000 copies each. She was invited by the Indian princely courts and paid a sum of 2,000 rupees for her performance.

She died in 1934 and willed her wealth to a trust to be used for the welfare of the poor and needy and public charity.

Sundra Bai of Pune (1885–1955)

Born in Pune in a poor family, Sundra Bai had no formal education but picked up folk music and bhajans and joined a troupe in Marathi theatre. After becoming famous in Maharashtra, she travelled to Delhi, Lucknow and Banaras, and learned Urdu and Hindi. She took lessons from Dhaman Khan, an accomplished tabla player, in light classical music—thumri, hori, kajri, chaiti and ghazal—and soon emerged as a high-ranking artist in Bombay music circles. She was even invited by the nizam to perform in his durbar at Hyderabad. She recorded about 180 songs on 100 78 rpm discs from pure classical ragas to thumris, ghazals and bhajans.

Kind-hearted and simple, Sundra Bai became wealthy but was deceived by unscrupulous people who set up a record company which failed completely and left her bankrupt. She was forced to seek employment at the Bombay Radio Station whose then director Z.A. Bokhari appointed her as an advisor. She continued to work there until her demise in 1953, by which time she was a forgotten artiste, no mention being made even of her end. Her songs continue to enchant music lovers.

Malika Pukhraj (1912–2004)

Born near Jammu, Malika Pukhraj was a child prodigy with a melodious voice. She learnt Urdu and Persian and was trained by Ustad Allah Bux, a maestro of classical music. She also learnt Kathak dance from Mamman Khan at Delhi. When she was just nine years old, she was invited to perform at the court of Maharaja Hari Singh at Jammu where she captivated everyone with her heavenly voice and rustic charm. The maharaja appointed her as a court singer. She was also a companion to the maharaja and stayed at the court for nearly ten years. A palace intrigue led to her leaving Jammu and she went to Lahore where her family established her as a *mehfil* singer. Pukhraj soon became famous and the Gramophone Company invited her for recording. She was also invited by the Lahore Radio to perform.

She had a unique style of rendering thumris, ghazals and folk songs, and attained countrywide fame with her timeless melody *Abhi toh main jawan hoon*, a poem by renowned Urdu poet Hafiz Jallandhri.

Malika had many admirers but she married a government official Shabbir Hussain Shah in defiance of her family. She stopped singing in *mehfil*s but continued to perform for the Radio and Gramophone Company. She received several awards and had fans all over the subcontinent. She passed way in February 2004 and left behind an informative and interesting autobiography written in Urdu. It was translated and published in India during her lifetime as *The Song Sung True* in 2003. Not just a remarkable life-story, this autobiography is a valuable piece of social history.

Akhtari Bai Fyzabadi (Begum Akhtar)

Akhtari Bai was born in 1914 at Fyzabad. She received her early training from Ata Mahammed Khan, stalwart of the Tanras *gharana* and from Ustad Immdad Khan, a noted sarangi exponent. After she moved to Calcutta with her mother, she had further training from famous classical maestros like Mohammed Khan and Abdul Wahid Khan, after which she became a disciple of Ustad Jhande Khan.

Akhtari's first stage performance at the tender age of fifteen in Calcutta took the music world by storm. She also cut her first gramophone disc *Diwana banana hai toh*, which created a sensation; this ghazal remains an all-time favourite. She was drawn to the film world also but gave it up after a few ventures. In 1943, Akhtari became a court singer at the palace of nawab of Rampur. Here she met Ishtiaq Ahmad Abassi whom she married in 1945 and came to be known as Begum Akhtar. As desired by her husband she stopped singing for nearly five years but fell ill and music was prescribed as her only cure. She resumed singing for the radio and public concerts which she continued until her demise in 1974. She became a legend in her own lifetime and *malika-e-ghazal* in the true sense.

Begum Akhtar had a magnetic personality and her mission in life was to regale her listeners with her soulful music. Her ghazal singing in fact carried the flavour and traits of K.L. Saigal. Perhaps the last singer from the clan of professional artistes, Begum Akhtar brought the ghazal *gayaki* from the *kotha* to the concert hall and was duly honoured by the government with prestigious awards. In her tribute to K.L. Saigal, she observed that many eminent artistes had sung ghazals but none could match the legendary Saigal's rendition of Ghalib.

Inayatbai Dherowali (1910–80)

In the early decades of the twentieth century, Lahore was the cultural hub of north India. Thanks to the generous patronage of the landed gentry and the princely states, there were famous ustads like Barkat Ali Khan and Bade Ghulam Ali Khan who trained young professional singing girls so they could entertain music lovers in their *kotha*s. Some highly accomplished ustads among them where invited by Lahore Radio and the HMV Gramophone Company.

Inayatbai was one such artiste. Born in the village Dherowal in 1910, she was trained by Ustad Bade Ghulam Ali Khan. Stunningly beautiful with a golden voice, she was a leading singer of her generation and was invited to perform in the durbars of the princely states of north India. A very popular singer of her time she was acclaimed in Lahore as *malika-e-ghazal* during the 1930s.

Zohra Bai Agrewali (1918–90)

Born in a family of professional musicians, Zohra Bai received training in classical music from early childhood. Endowed with a sweet and sonorous voice, Zohra Bai climbed the ladder of fame and popularity. She made her debut at the age of thirteen and the Gramophone Company cut her first disc in 1932, which won the appreciation of music lovers. She was soon recognized as an accomplished exponent of light classical music, thumri, dadra and ghazal. HMV brought out several records of Zohra Bai's songs which had a ready market.

During the 1940s Zohra Bai emerged as a leading playback singer in the Bombay film industry. Famous music composer Naushad Ali exploited Zohra's talent in the superhit *Rattan* in 1944. Zohra's zesty rendering of *Akhian mila ke jiya bharmake* and other numbers won her

Zohra Bai Agrewali

countrywide fame and turned her into a celebrity in the music world. At the zenith of her fame in the 1940s, her songs in a film would ensure its success at the box office. However her film career was brief, just under a decade. She spent her last few years in semi-retirement and passed away in 1990.

The Artiste and
the Man

Acclaimed as the greatest performing artiste of the twentieth century, K.L. Saigal inspired a generation of Indian singers, including Surendra, Mohammad Rafi, Mukesh, Kishore Kumar and C.H. Atma. Neither a torchbearer of any *gharana*, nor a *shagird* of any eminent ustad, Saigal was a self-taught singer with an instinctive knowledge of the ragas, imbibed by listening to a wide range of singers. With his divine voice, Saigal created a singular place for himself in the world of Indian music.

Before he joined the film industry in Calcutta, Saigal would sing at private gatherings, as mentioned by eminent singer Pahari Sanyal, who was later his colleague at the New Theatres. He described a musical soirée at his friend's house at Moradabad where everyone, agog with excitement, was talking about the highly talented new singer who was coming that evening to regale the audience. For Sanyal, this was the first occasion to hear Saigal sing. Later, when Sanyal heard him on the screen in the New Theatres' *Dulari Bibi*, a two-reeler film, he realized that Saigal's voice through the loudspeaker was much sweeter than without one, as at the parties. This exceptional suitability of his voice to the microphone proved to him that Saigal was indeed a rare specimen of natural singer whose singing remained entirely effortless. Sanyal also emphasized that he never heard Saigal go out of tune.

Saigal's film music was largely moulded and groomed by New Theatres' stalwarts like R.C. Boral and Pankaj Mullick. Mullick, who was Saigal's friend, appreciated his talent and his extraordinary ability to sing ghazals, bhajans and thumris with equal ease and brilliance.

He attributed Saigal's phenomenal success, his countrywide fame and popularity to his own special talent and effort. He said, 'Saigal's music had always seemed so natural that no one thought there was anything more to it than the ability to speak with a little tune to it. It took more than a generation to discover that this kind of singing was the result of excruciating labour. A mere good voice is just not enough . . . what is happening to Saigal is that over the years he has become in a certain sense a musician's musician. It is truly ironic that a singer who was supposed to know nothing of ragas and was not formally trained should be perceived as a musician's musician. When he sang, an essence came through the song which cast a spell on the listener; it was the *swara* that emerged from his being.'

Much has been said about Saigal's voice. We have another account of circumstances that led to the emergence of Saigal's unique voice as an ideal one for the microphone. According to Boral, when Saigal began singing for *Devdas*, his voice cracked because of a sore throat. The recording was postponed but his sore throat persisted for a while. Finally, Saigal tried to sing in a soft tone, which admirably suited the ambience Barua was trying to create. It also agreed with the volume requirements of the microphone and soundtrack. This time it showed no crack and Boral instructed the sound man to record the song in that style. The result was more than gratifying, and Saigal developed a penchant for singing in a soft voice. This is one of the explanations given for the special singing style that soon became Saigal's trademark. Another popular theory traces the origin of Saigal's vocal style to his singing in *Dushman* where he plays the role of a TB patient. It is pointed out that in his early films, such as *Puran Bhakt* and *Yahoodi ki Ladki*, Saigal sang with a resonant, natural open-throated voice but later developed the soft, soothing tone which eventually became his hallmark.

One more explanation attributes the special mellowness of his voice to his fondness for liquor and this view is endorsed by some of his contemporaries. But this has little bearing when discussing an artiste of Saigal's calibre. All the same, the claim that out of the two or three recordings sung by Saigal, the one sung in his sober mood was much better than the other one sung while he was under the influence of liquor is not true. That this impression is mere gossip is substantiated by G.N. Joshi, a senior executive of HMV in Bombay for over thirty

In *Dushman*

years who personally handled Saigal's recordings. He writes in *Down Melody Lane*:

> While working in the Ranjit film company, he frequently came to our studio to record his songs, always in the afternoon. On

arrival, he would come straight to my cabin and put his bottle of scotch in my table drawer. He knew very well that it was safe with me!

Normally, there would be about half a dozen rehearsals before the actual recording. He would have half a peg between rehearsals. His voice became mellower with each rehearsal, and then would come a stage that was the ultimate in beauty. It was my job to catch him on disc at this stage, when every word, every note bore the stamp of rare and rich artistry. All the songs he recorded for *Tansen*, *Surdas* and *Shah Jehan* became immortal.

Joshi had known Saigal since 1935 when he met him at the Allahabad music conference. He adds: 'Saigals's devotion to his work was far above any other artiste's. He had a heart of gold and was a faithful friend. He never turned away a needy fellow artist. On several occasions, I saw him dig into his pocket and give away all he had to some unfortunate person.'

Saigal's was a voice which played with the mystery and soul of a song and produced everything the music director wanted. He decorated words with music and had the gift of singing a single line in more than twenty different ways, evoking corresponding moods and feelings. The magical spell of his singing led the audience to another cosmic domain.

Music, according to E.M. Forster, is of two types. To him one was music that reminded him of 'something' while the other was music itself. K.L. Saigal embodied the latter variety. His voice had an echo which stirred the listener to feel it was travelling to the horizon, from one end to the other, like the rising sun. Listeners are transported to another world of spirit and philosophy on hearing *Na main kisi ka, na koi mera*, *Kisne ye sab khel rachaya*, *Bina pankh panchhi hun mai*, *Bina pankh panchhi hun mai* and *Toot gaye sab sapne mere*. What Saigal really does is touch our heartstrings. Another striking feature of his voice was that it changed from song to song. The voice that sang *Babul mora* was not the same in that famous lullaby *So ja rajkumari*, or in his maiden recording *Jhulana jhulavo*. There are several instances of this phenomenon; his speech and song merged into each other.

According to Pahari Sanyal, Bengali songs probably brought out the best in Saigal. He was the first non-Bengali artist who put new life into Bengali songs as no Bengali songster ever could or did. He was

In *Dushman* with Jagdish Sethu

particularly inspired by Tagore's songs. And even his imperfect Bengali accent charmed listeners and he became a darling of the Bengalis, more than any Bengali artiste.

There is little written material on Saigal's life; no diaries, letters, interviews or media coverage. Only the bits and pieces his contemporaries, friends and colleagues said in their writings or interviews can be gleaned. Saigal is said to have been a perfect gentleman, full of humility and compassion. Generous to the core, there are several anecdotes of his giving away everything he had, including clothes, to the poor and needy. His salary was collected by his family directly from the New Theatres' office lest he part with it on his way home. Once, he is said to have given away his diamond ring to a widow in distress at Poona. Another fine trait was that he remained unaffected by his success, fame and popularity. He was hardly even conscious of the fact that he had become a successful star. He was affable and affectionate and made no distinction between people based on rank or class. A sufi at heart, he was humane and sensitive and could sense the pain, sorrow and suffering of others. He

Saigal giving Kanan Bala music lessons in *Street Singer*

was unconventional in his way of life. Though it is uncorroborated, it is said that Saigal was not allowed to marry the girl he loved, a princess from Assam. He took to drink, staying within limits possibly due to his ailments.

Saigal kept indifferent health but rarely talked about his personal problems. He never criticized or spoke ill of anybody. None of his contemporaries ever saw him lose his temper. He was a private person and never opened his heart to anyone including members of his family. For him, singing was not just a profession; it was a passion and his life's mission. Back home from the studio, he never talked about it and seldom saw his own films. According to Chaman Puri, who acted with Saigal in *Street Singer* and was his greatest admirer, the best place for Saigal was the home and the family. He would often hold singing *mehfil*s where he would play his harmonium and the others joined him. But he never allowed anyone to speak about his work and studio.

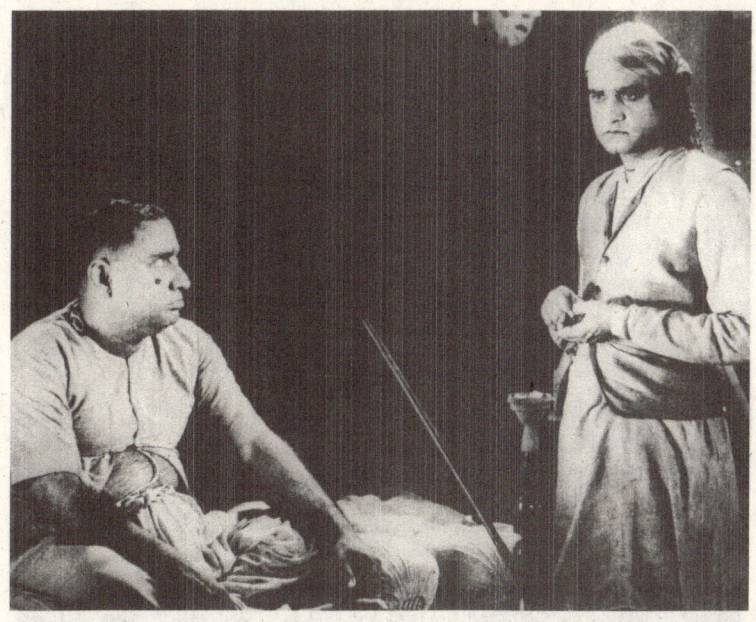

A scene from *Street Singer*

In *Street Singer*

A scene from *My Sister*

My Sister

Saigal's great interest in cooking is mentioned in several contemporary accounts. Pankaj Mullick is said to have enjoyed the dishes which he brought to the studio for his friends. He was fond of delicacies such as

Saigal with Kanan Bala in *Street Singer*

meat dishes in the Mughlai style, full of chillies and spices. He ate pickles, *pakora*s and chutney, regardless of their effect on his vocal chords. He also enjoyed smoking cigarettes, which he carried in his cigarette case. Fortunately, his voice remained unaffected and its range and pathos continued to cast their spell until the end.

Saigal was both a simple and highly complex personality. He had little interest in his publicity and praise. An introvert, he was also shy of speaking about himself and his achievements. He only relaxed and enjoyed himself in the company of his limited intimate circle of friends. If anyone applauded and complimented him on his song he would laugh it away and retort, *Kerah koi sher mar laya, ik geet ee gaya na, chhad yar* (I have not killed a lion, just a song, forget about it). At home, he enjoyed chatting and joking with family members of all age groups. His daughter, Bina Chopra, once told me that she remembered her father bringing a battery-operated toy train for her which he assembled himself and made it run on the track, enjoying the whole incident with her in his lap.

Saigal with Sumitra Devi in *My Sister*

Another admirable trait in Saigal's character was his complete devotion, respect and affection for his parents. Pahari Sanyal makes a special mention about his deep attachment to his mother who could make him do things at the slightest gesture or word from her. Sanyal also appreciated the way he looked after his visiting relations and family friends. He would himself travel in a tram and give his luxury car to his guests. Pankaj also mentioned Saigal's great devotion to his wife and children.

Saigal had a great regard for his fellow artistes and went out of the way to help them. The late Kidar Sharma spoke in a television interview about Saigal's kind and generous nature and how he helped him arrange his meeting with B.N. Sircar. Also, when Jaddan Bai, mother of superstar Nargis, was struggling in Calcutta, it was Saigal who after noticing her talent as a singer encouraged and convinced her that there was a whole world to be won with her melodies. So, from a gramophone singer, Jaddan Bai became an actress, music director and film producer.

Saigal was reserved and pensive by nature. Absorbed in his own thoughts, he was oblivious to the happenings around him. There is an amusing episode told by Phani Majumdar, the creator of *Street Singer* and a great admirer of Saigal. He noticed that Saigal once bought a motorcycle but refused to ride it himself and hired a driver to take him around. Finally, he got a licence and began riding it himself. But he was not confident about his driving and was always looking towards the tram terminus, only a few furlongs from New Theatres, for colleagues from the studio.

One day, he offered Pankaj Mullick a ride on his bike as he drove to the studio. Phani Majumdar had seen Pankaj on the pillion seat but when he reached the office, he noticed Saigal was alone on his bike. Not only was Saigal unaware of when Pankaj fell off from the pillion on the way, he did not even recall having offered a ride to Pankaj.

Phani Majumdar rated Saigal as an artiste of rare quality, a great actor and singer, and also a very dear and respected friend. He was so good that the camera could linger on his face even when someone else was delivering the dialogue. Saigal was always willing to listen to his director, no matter who he was, and did precisely as told. Majumdar refers to the recording of the famous song *Babul mora* in *Street Singer*, an outstanding example of Saigal's talents both as an actor and as a singer.

The playback system was already established by then. But Saigal did not want the authenticity of the scene to be diluted in any way. He requested Majumdar to make it a direct take and assured him that the result would be better than a playback version. It was difficult to shoot the song live on the roads, but Saigal was completely immersed in the song and the role. Majumdar says, 'I don't think any other actor could have done it so well.'

The eminent playback singer of yesteryears, Rajkumari, was thrilled when she got the opportunity to sing with K.L. Saigal. She says: 'I admired him tremendously. We sang that lovely naughty duet in *Bhakt Surdas*, *Sar pe kadam ki chhaiyan muraliya bag rahi*. I remember him saying to me, "Rajkumari I have something to say to you. I want to take you with me when I go up." Unfortunately I did not get to sing with him again.'

Another episode related by Majumdar is about Saigal's role in Barua's *Devdas*. When Saigal requested Majumdar to help him at his rehearsal, he agreed to do so on the condition that Saigal would sing a song for him each time he retired to his make-up room—and he cheerfully kept his word. Jamini Roy, the renowned painter who had known Saigal from his earlier days in New Theatres, once said, 'He was such a pure character, so simple that it is hard to describe him in simple words. He was like somebody who had stepped out of an icon so unaffected, totally oblivious of himself, like a line drawing.'

Saigal's son, the late Madan Mohan, talked about his father in an interview with a Hindi magazine in 1973 at Bombay. 'My father did drink like anybody else. In the case of film personalities, there is always undue noise and gossip. No one bothers how much one takes. I still remember him pouring whisky from his silver flask in a silver tumbler, mixing water instead of soda. While he enjoyed his drink, my sister and I used to take music lessons in his presence from our teacher Jagan Nath Prasad. He would then listen to our practice. I did not see him drinking in excess at home. Nor do I remember his ever coming home in a drunken state.'

Madan Mohan also said that his father was a deeply religious person. Every morning he would sit in the balcony with his harmonium and elatedly sing two bhajans—*Utho sonewalo sahar ho gayi hai, utho rat sari basar ho gayi hai* (It is already morning, so wake up from your slumber, as the night is over) and the other one was *Pee le re tu oh matwala, hari nam ka payala* (Don't lose your senses, but surrender yourself and drink the nectar of devotion to Lord Hari). Madan Mohan showed a silver teaset presented to Saigal by Morris College students and a certificate by the Bengal Music Association for his proficiency as a Bengali singer. He also mentioned that his father's favourite singer was Abdul Karim Khan.

Eminent music director Naushad also bears out Saigal's spiritual leanings. He says that before every formal occasion of singing Saigal would say a prayer with his *mala*, something Naushad noticed during one of his recordings for *Shah Jehan*.

Naushad respected Saigal not only as a great artiste but also as a great man. It was his greatness that had attracted Dr Latif who had no ear for music but left his medical practice and family in Calcutta to stay with Saigal in Bombay to attend to his health. He gave him medical attention day and night at the sets while shooting was on. Naushad was deeply touched when Latif told him, 'Saigal is a very good man and a great friend who needs understanding.'

Singing in *My Sister*

Over the years, Saigal's fan following spread all over the country and he received voluminous fan mail, but he is reported to have said, 'I don't reply to letters. I hardly read them.' But he welcomed every visitor, even a stranger, who called on him.

There is a graphic account of his last days in Jullundur as narrated by Saigal's sister-in-law, the wife of his elder brother, over twenty years ago to the eminent Punjabi writer, Balwant Gargi. According to her, Kundan was a great soul . . . very generous, an unusual person. He was ill and in need of complete rest but would tell us jokes and make us laugh. A few days before his death he had had his head shaved and said that he wanted to look like a sadhu and that on his return to Bombay he would play the roles of sadhus and *bhakt*s. But this was not to be. His condition became critical and he died on the morning of 18 January 1947, leaving behind his eternal melodies for hordes of his mourners in the country.

Saigal's Heroines

Saigal appeared in a span of about fifteen years in twenty-eight Hindi films and a few Bengali films. His career was primarly connected with New Theatres of Calcutta, which was then hailed as the most progressive studio of the country.

During the silent era, the first women to join films were Anglo-Indians. But after the advent of sound, as they were not fluent in Hindi and Urdu, they lost their position in the industry. This opened up new opportunities for professional artistes, especially those trained in dance and music.

Saigal's first heroine was Rattan Bai, a famous professional singer of the time. Originally called Imam Bandhi, she had received training in classical music from accomplished ustads of music. She had a charming face and was known for her extraordinarily long hair, which was said to have reached near her ankles. Their first film was *Subah ki Sitara* (1932), directed by Nitin Bose with R.C. Boral's music. A popular song by Rattan Bai was *Hato jao, na humko satayo ji*. The hit song by Saigal was *Khuli hai botal, bharen hain sagar, sharab mehfil mein chal rahi hai*. The film was not a great success and just managed to break even. Their second film together, *Yahoodi ki Ladki* (1933) directed by Premankur Atorthy with music by stalwarts Boral and Mullick proved to be a notable success. The film had nineteen songs, most of which became popular, including Rattan Bai's hit number *Apnem maula ki jogan banungi, viyogan banungi*.

The next film in which Rattan Bai co-starred with Saigal as a supporting heroine, along with Rajkumari, was *Karwan-e-Hayat* (1935), released after the historic *Devdas*. An adventure movie where Rattan Bai plays the role of a gypsy girl falling in love with a romantic prince (Saigal) in disguise, was quite successful, with some popular songs by

Rattan Bai in *Roop Lekha*

the duo, including Rattan Bai's *Ishq bina kya jeevan ka sukh, dil ka chain hai ulfat ka dukh*.

During the 1930s, the actresses usually expected to sing were usually drawn from families of established professional singers who had earlier provided artistes to theatrical companies. Acting was not then treated as a respectable profession for young women and even for men from educated middle-class families. These women artistes, like Rattan Bai and her contemporaries, including Miss Kajjan, Mukhtar Begum, Jaddan Bai and Indubala, belonged to a class of artistes who carried on their hereditary profession of dance and music. They appeared in different incarnations as *ganika*s, *nartaki*s, *devadasi*s, *kanchani*s and *tawaif*s, preserving through centuries our traditional performing arts of music and dance.

Rattan Bai disappeared from the scene after 1935 and did not appear in any of the New Theatres' productions. But in December 1937, when Saigal was invited to Lahore by the All-India Exhibition organizers, her name was among the artistes invited from different parts of India

Uma Shashi in *Dharti Mata*

With Leela Desai in *President*

to perform at the Exhibition Theatre. It is most likely that the kind-hearted and generous Saigal might have recommended her name for her participation there. Perhaps her last appearance was a secondary role in *Sitara* (1939), produced by Everest Pictures of Bombay.

Saigal's second heroine who sang that famous duet with him, *Prem nagar mein banaungi ghar main*, was Uma Shashi in *Chandidas*, a box-office hit of 1934. She joined Saigal once again as the leading lady in *Dharti Mata* where Saigal dominates the film with his songs but Uma Shashi also swayed the audience with her memorable chorus, *Duniya rang rangili baba* and her lively duet with Saigal, *Main man ki baat bataun*.

Jamuna, the immortal Parbati of *Devdas*, was Saigal's next heroine. She also co-starred with Barua in the Bengali version. Both Saigal and Jamuna achieved superstardom with their outstanding performances in *Devdas*. Jamuna was no singer but Barua had picked her up from a chorus dancing group and groomed her into an accomplished and sensitive artiste. He succeeded in embellishing her with the high personal

With Kamlesh Kumari in *President*

integrity of Parbati and created a cult figure of her along with Saigal, who earned the title of tragedy king after virtually living the role of Devdas. Barua successfully cast her once again with Saigal after a lapse of five years in *Zindagi* (1940). Here he showed Saigal living with a married woman with his platonic love and Jamuna's performance was quite extraordinary and impressive. Barua took Jamuna as his second wife and left New Theatres in 1941. He set up his own production unit but his only successful feature film was *Jawab* (1942) where Jamuna played a supporting role as the film was dominated by Kanan Bala's superb acting and her enchanting music. Between *Devdas* and *Zindagi*, Saigal co-starred with Leela Desai playing the heroine in two successive hits, *President* and *Dushman*. Both these films carried delightful melodies by Saigal solo as Leela Desai was not a singer though an accomplished dancer as portrayed in *Dushman*. Later, Leela Desai went on an all-India tour and gave dance performances on the stage. I vividly recall having seen her performance at the Regent Cinema of Lahore.

Now we come to the queen of melody of Indian cinema, the greatest singer–actress of all times, the illustrious Kanan (Bala) Devi (1916–92), an amateur singer when she joined cinema. She received training in classical music from Allah Rakha, an eminent ustad of Lucknow. This qualified and equipped her to master light classical, or semi-classical,

Leela Desai in *Dushman*

Kamlesh Kumari in *President*

including the ghazal form of singing. She learnt Rabindra Sangeet from
Anade Dastidar, *kirtan* from Dhirendra Mitra and *nazrul geeti* from
Kazi Nazrul Islam. As she writes in her autobiography *Sabre Ami Nomi*,
she was invited by Gurudev Tagore to Shantiniketan to learn Rabindra
Sangeet, which she considered a matter of great honour for her. But,
above all, her real teacher was New Theatres' R.C. Boral, considered the
father of Indian film music. Barua was very particular that Kanan play the

role of Parbati in his *Devdas* but her contract with Radha Film Company prevented her from doing so. Later, however, she joined New Theatres and Debaki Bose gave her the leading role in his masterpiece *Vidyapati* (1937). Kanan dominates the film with her intense performance. Her catchy, tuneful songs along with lively duets with K.C. Dey made her the top star of the New Theatres. She followed it up as a leading lady in Barua's *Mukti*, again an astounding success which established her as a singing superstar. Finally, it is as Saigal's heroine in that historic movie *Street Singer* (1938) that Kanan emerged as the melody queen and reached the zenith of her fame and popularity. The Saigal–Kanan team mesmerized the audience not only with their glorious duets and respective solos, but also with their fantastic true-to-life performances. In the process, they immortalized themselves as the greatest singing-duo in the country. The public had never before seen Saigal act in such a relaxed and natural way. *Street Singer* surpassed in its pristine musical beauty and the flood of song and melody earlier great hits like *Vidyapati* and *Mukti*. Kanan's superb performance acquired a halo; it was said that she had honey in her throat and her rich, resonant, full voice enchanted the audiences already enthralled with Saigal's golden voice. Saigal and Kanan had a deep and genuine admiration for each other's talents.

Street Singer proved to be the 'New Theatres' greatest musical extravaganza with its eternal melody *Babul mora naihar chhuto he jaye*. Kanan co-starred with Saigal once again in *Lagan* (1941) with a good bunch of songs—four by Kanan and five by Saigal—which contributed in no small measure to its commercial success. Soon after, Saigal left for Bombay to work for Ranjit Studios and Kanan joined P.C. Barua's own venture, MP Productions.

Another heroine from Calcutta to work with Saigal was Sumitra Devi in *My Sister* (1944). The film's success was largely attributed to Saigal's very popular songs composed by Pankaj Mullick. Sumitra had a beautiful face but little talent in music. She later joined Bombay Talkies and appeared in a few films. She was not able to make any mark in the profession though she co-starred with famous stars such as Ashok Kumar and Kishore Sahu.

Saigal's next heroine, who really inspired and animated the singer in him, was the then-leading singing actress of Bombay, Khurshid. She had already earned name and fame in several hits of Ranjit Studios, including *Holi, Musafir* (1940), *Pardesi* and *Shadi* (1941). Hailing from

Kanan Devi

Lahore, she began her career in Abdul Rashid Kardar's silent films and her first talkie was J.K. Nanda's *Swarg ki Seedhi* made at Lahore in 1935. She became a known star only after her appearance in *Sitara* (1939) directed by Ezra Mir. A charming personality with an extraordinary acting talent, Khurshid was an accomplished singer too. Like Saigal, she had a Punjabi background and outlook.

Khurshid was overjoyed when Ranjit Studios decided to cast her with him in *Bhakt Surdas* (1942). The film was a runaway success and the Saigal–Khurshid team suddenly shot into the limelight and achieved all-India fame and popularity.

This was followed by *Tansen* (1943), an even bigger box-office hit. Khurshid, with her lively, unrestrained performance and lilting voice, seemed to have been a natural heroine to co-star with Saigal. On his part, Saigal, too, gave the impression of being perfectly at ease with Khurshid and his performance was both natural and spontaneous. Apart from the remarkable singing abilities of the duo, credit should also go to the highly talented music director Khemchand Prakash who composed the music for *Tansen*. It is the same Khemchand who was to create a sensation later in 1949 with his fantastic melody *Ayega aane wala* of *Mahal* and in the process launched Lata Mangeshkar as a leading playback singer. After Partition, Khurshid, who had married actor Lala Yakub, left for Pakistan where she made only two films, both in 1956, before retiring. She died in April 2001 in Karachi.

Saigal's last surviving heroine, Suraiya, died on 31 January 2004. Born in Lahore in 1929, Suraiya began her career as a child-artiste in *Taj Mahal* (1941). Naushad Ali, the famous composer, discovered her singing talent and gave her a chance to sing playback for Mehtab in the film *Sharda* (1942). She was just thirteen years old and had to stand on a stool to sing the famous hit *Panchhi ja peeche raha hai bachpan*. No one could imagine that this simple young girl, without any training in classical music, would one day emerge as the leading singing superstar. By the age of fifteen, she was already a singing actress with notable success in the Bombay Talkies' *Hamari Baat* (1943). During the mid-1940s, Suraiya along with the famous Noor Jahan dominated the film world as singing-actresses.

It is said that K.L. Saigal was favourably impressed by Suraiya's voice and recommended her to Jayant Desai, who had booked Saigal for his planned production of *Tadbir* (1945). Jayant was already satisfied with her role in his just-completed big budget historical, *Samrat*

Khurshid

Suraiya

Chandragupta. So, Suraiya was teamed up with Saigal in *Tadbir* even before her remarkable achievement in Mehboob's famous hit *Anmol Ghadi*. She followed it up with two more films as Saigal's heroine in *Omar Khayyam* and *Parwana* (1947). Suraiya is the only artiste who has acted with Saigal in three films. It is a pity that with the exception of *Parwana*, the other two films though enriched with songs did not make any impact. The nominal success of *Parwana* was largely due its release after Saigal's premature death in January 1947. Multitudes of Saigal's admirers and devout fans crowded the theatres everywhere to see *Parwana* merely to pay their homage to the memory of the immortal singer. For Suraiya, it was no doubt a matter of pride to be known as the last heroine of the legendary singer–actor.

A few years ago, while paying homage to her great hero, Suraiya said that Saigal treated her like a daughter and her mother as a sister and it was he who had suggested to Mohan Sinha to sign her for *Omar Khayyam*. Later, according to Suraiya, she was scheduled to act with Saigal in *Meri Surat Teri Ankhen* but on learning that the heroine had been changed, Saigal declined to act in the film. Suraiya was very moved by the gesture; she had held Saigal in high esteem and regarded him as a great soul and a perfect gentleman.

Saigal's Mentors
and Associates

Saigal's foremost mentor was the illustrious founder of the New Theatres, B.N. Sircar (1901–80). The son of Sir N.N. Sircar, the law member of the Viceroy's Council, B.N. Sircar qualified as an engineer from England but was drawn to the world of cinema, setting up his studio in February 1931. Polished, suave and soft-spoken, he collected a team of talented directors and technicians but his initial ventures in Bengali and Urdu films were not successful. He had no interest in being a performer or a director, wanting only to be a creative producer of films. His determination and vision soon brought him rewards with the astounding success of his *Chandidas* in Bengali. Thereafter, there was no looking back and the next decade was to be dominated by the 'trumpeting elephant', the inspiring logo of New Theatres. Sircar turned his studio into an institution of academic importance, setting up new aesthetic standards to enrich the form and content of Indian cinema. He emerged as a pioneer in the finest sense of the term and achieved his goal as a creative genius by transforming film production into a work of art with its own identity. His films from *Puran Bhakt* to *Hamrahi* projected contemporary social issues. In many respects, they were much ahead of their times and served as a beaconlight to the other film producers in the country. Sircar would sit in his office under a thatched roof on the lawns called 'Gol Ghar' and coordinate activities.

He created a friendly atmosphere and made everyone feel like a member of a large family. A man of vision and understanding, he had once said, 'I do not make films only to make profits.' Even after New Theatres closed down, Sircar, as president of the Film Federation of

India, the apex body in the country at the time, devoted himself to the progress and development of the film industry at a national level.

Saigal owed his first successful appearance in a film to Debaki Bose (1898–1971), the legendary director of New Theatres and the creator of *Puran Bhakt*, the great hit which set a new milestone in Indian cinema with its aesthetic approach. Debaki Bose came to films via the freedom movement. He had edited a national weekly *Shakti* and after working as a scriptwriter and director of two silent films, in 1932 he joined New Theatres. Bose exploited the rich mythological literature and history of India for his thematic material but gave an intensely human touch to his characters.

He was the only New Theatres' director to work on a contract basis and was free to make films for other producers. He built his reputation on the basis of his artistic taste, warm humanity and high standard of work, enriched with innovations. His masterpiece *Seeta*, which he made for the East India Film Company, won him international acclaim. It was the first Indian film to be shown at the Vienna Film Festival in 1934 and was hailed as the best mythological film ever made. Then, in 1937, he brought fame to New Theatres with his classic *Vidyapati*, for which he was the scriptwriter as well as the director.

Photograph taken in 1938, when Sir Sikandar Hayat, chief minister of undivided Punjab, visited New Theatres.

He was a pioneer in many ways and brought to Indian films his special philosophy, art, poetry and a certain dignity which the audience responded to. He introduced a fresh concept of movie-making, which inspired several other filmmakers. Saigal came under Bose's influence when he used his singing talent in the films *Rajrani Meera* and *Dulari Bibi*.

Another director who groomed Saigal into a cult figure was the noble prince of Gauripur and renowned creative genius, Pramathesh Chandra Barua (1903–51). A young intellectual, Barua had studied art in Paris, where he was drawn to the cinema. He set up his own production unit in Calcutta and made a few silent films, including the famous Debaki Bose-directed *Apradhi*, in which Barua himself had the leading role.

After meeting B.N. Sircar, Barua joined New Theatres and soon achieved unprecedented fame and popularity with his all-time classic, *Devdas*. He became a living legend in Bengal filmdom. He was not only a

Debaki Bose

Nitin Bose

great actor and director but also an outstanding philosopher. Handsome, talented and rich, he was the heart-throb of millions. He had the capacity to draw the best performances from his actors and actresses. He pulled Jamuna out from a chorus group and, Pygmalion-like, built her up into a consummate actress and an all-India star. His later films—*Manzil*, *Mukti* and *Adhikar*—were great hits, the last one being rated as the best picture of 1938. But one of his greatest films and the last one for New Theatres was *Zindagi* (1940) where he also handled the camera. Later, he went freelance and his most famous film, *Jawab* (1942), was produced and directed by him with Kanan, Jamuna and himself in the lead.

   Though not in the same league as Debaki Bose and Barua, Nitin Bose (1897–1986) began his career as a cameraman and shot many films for Debaki Bose. Grandson of Sir J.C. Bose and cousin of Satyajit

Pankaj Mullick

Ray, Nitin had his directorial debut in 1933 when Debaki Bose left the studio. He followed in the footsteps of his mentor Debaki Bose and his first feature film was the remake of *Chandidas* in Hindi. Nitin was a visionary who pre-empted the mores of modern filmmaking and is acknowledged for his pioneering role in introducing the 'playback' as early as 1935 in *Dhoop Chhaon* even before it was introduced

Pahari Sanyal

in America. Pankaj Mullick, in May 1935, became the world's first playback singer.

Nitin was also responsible for introducing the technique of filming sequences. All his later films—*President*, *Dushman* and *Dharmatma*—with Saigal in the lead were highly successful and established him as another stalwart of New Theatres. Nitin was a master craftsman of his art who understood the importance of film as a medium of creative expression and knew how to excel in it.

Naushad

There was a special affinity between Bose and Saigal. According to Vivek Benegal's tribute to him carried by the *Telegraph* in 1986, Nitin had promised Saigal a role in each of his films, but Pahari Sanyal bagged the role in both the Hindi and the Bengali versions of *Dhoop Chhaon*. According to Nitin, Saigal was so hurt by what he took to be rejection, that he, who never drank up until then, took his first drink, marking the beginning of an abiding habit. Nitin was burdened with guilt.

Another interesting anecdote relates to the New Theatres' practice of making films in two versions, in Hindi and in Bengali. Once, Saigal announced that he wanted to play both versions planned by Nitin Bose. When it was pointed out to him that he knew no Bengali, Saigal

Phani Majumdar

Khemchand Prakash

R.C. Boral

Jaddan Bai

A.R. Kardar

Chandulal J. Shah

surprised the director by speaking in fluent Bengali. He had been studying Bengali.

Nitin left for Bombay in 1941 and made a number of successful films there, including *Ganga Jumna* (1961), but missed Bengal and often even regretted his decision of leaving Calcutta.

Saigal's mentor in Bombay was Chandulal J. Shah, a leading director and producer and the founder of the famous Ranjit Studios. Shah had begun his career as a stockbroker but was drawn to the film-world in the silent era and directed a number of films which were highly successful in those days. His best-known film was *Gun Sundri* which was remade in 1934 as a talkie. With Shah as the head of the studio, Ranjit set up an assembly-line approach to filmmaking and continued to be the country's largest film producer until 1950. In 1941 Shah persuaded Saigal to come to Bombay and made an agreement with him to appear in three films for him—*Bhakt Surdas*, *Tansen* and *Bhanwara*. However, with the changing times and the new generation of filmmakers and stars, Shah lost in the

Jayant Desai

race but remained an active leader of the film industry and was the first president of the Film Federation of India.

Saigal's last great hit, *Shah Jehan* (1946), was produced by Abdul Rashid Kardar, the famous movie mogul of his time. Hailing from Lahore, he was a pioneer from the silent era who gave us some immortal personalities and films took Hindi cinema to great heights. Kardar made more than forty films of all genres—musicals, romances, historical and costume dramas. A pioneer in many respects, Kardar had a fine ear for music. He gave Naushad a break and contributed to his later success as an eminent music director.

Saigal's film career in Bombay was not as successful. Except for *Bhakt Surdas* and *Tansen*, all the other Saigal films produced in Bombay went unnoticed and flopped at the box office. Kardar, however, succeeded in reviving Saigal's fading image due to his poor health and presented his masterpiece *Shah Jehan*, a symbol of Saigal's memory as an immortal singer.

Among Saigal's associates in Calcutta was everyone who worked in those days at the New Theatres' studio. According to contemporary accounts, Saigal was very friendly and everybody, both his superiors and juniors, was fond of him. Kidar Sharma had made reference to how Saigal went out of his way to help his friends.

Among his other close contacts was Prithviraj Kapoor, who co-starred with him in *Rajrani Meera*, *President* and *Dushman*, Jagdish Sethi, K.N. Singh, Pahari Sanyal and Pankaj Mullick. Some of them had already moved to Bombay before he went there. Like Nitin Bose, Saigal too missed his friends and associates in Calcutta where he had spent the best part of his professional life.

It could never be the same in Bombay and this eventually probably hastened his ultimate end.

Last Phase

As the Second World War dragged on, there was a boom in the film industry and several new producers appeared on the scene, especially in Bombay where processing laboratories and other technical facilities were now well-established. New Theatres, with its old captive audience of the educated middle-class, began losing its supremacy and two of its most talented directors, P.C. Barua and Nitin Bose, left the Company in late 1941. Some of Saigal's other colleagues—Prithviraj Kapoor, Jagdish Sethi, Kidar Sharma and K.N. Singh—had already left for Bombay.

Chandulal Shah, the chief of Ranjit Movietone and the industry's leader, made an attractive offer to Saigal to work in three films for a remuneration of over a lakh of rupees. It was a fabulous sum in those days; Saigal was at the time drawing a monthly salary of around 1,800 rupees under a contract with New Theatres. Sircar, the head of New Theatres, was extremely fond of Saigal and understood his circumstances. He was gracious enough to ignore Saigal's contractual obligations and allowed him to go to Bombay.

It may be recalled that earlier, K.D. Mehra, the father of the Punjabi film industry, had wanted Saigal to play the title role in *Heer Ranjha*, a popular love legend of Punjab. But Saigal could not take it up as it was not a New Theatres' picture.

The film scene in Bombay at that time was dominated by Bombay Talkies' hat-trick with *Kangan*, *Bandhan* and *Jhoola*, the last-named film then running to packed houses. The Ashok Kumar–Leela Chitnis pair had attained all-India fame and popularity and they followed it up by visiting the metropolitan cities and appearing on the cinema stage

116

to greet the hordes of their fans. I vividly recall their visit to Lahore and the way they were received at the railway station by thousands of young fans. All three films were conventional romantic melodramas in rural settings, artistically handled by S. Mukherjee, with simplified Hindustani dialogues and catchy songs. Even Ashok Kumar was hailed as a singer with the hits *Chal chal re naujawan* and *Na jane kidhar aaj meri nav chali re*.

Saigal arrived in Bombay late in 1941 and rented a flat in the college street of Matunga, a Bombay suburb where some of his old Calcutta friends also lived. His first film was *Bhakt Surdas* (1942), the story of the blind poet-saint. Directed by Chaturbhuj Doshi, and with its time-tested plot, it was a roaring success. Saigal and the heroine Khurshid, embellished the film with their delightful solos and duets in a feast of music.

Saigal had no rivals in Bombay, as the latter-day playback singers were still not on the horizon. Saigal's first film in Bombay established his supremacy which was to last till his final days. The music for *Bhakt Surdas* by Gyan Dutt was quite compatible with the theme. It is well accepted that Indian culture and tradition inspire the expression of feelings and emotions, joys and sorrows through song and dance as does the worship of the Lord through devotional music. Even though Gyan Dutt was not much appreciated for some of his compositions in the film, it was recognized that when Saigal sang them, listeners could not help being charmed. Besides, Saigal's portrayal of the saint-poet cast a magic spell on the viewers as *Bhakt Surdas* had made a home in every Hindu heart for generations. The songs of the film were penned by Madhok who gave such popular hits as *Sar pe kadam ki chhaiyan, Nayan heen ko rah dikha prabhu* and *Madhukar sham hamare chor*. Saigal also sang the most famous and popular Surdas bhajan—*Main nahin makhan khayo*—in his own *swara* and style which had a greater appeal than the rendition of the same bhajan by other eminent classical singers of the time.

In the beginning, Saigal felt like an exile in Bombay. He missed the artistic and cultural ambience of New Theatres. Being an intensely private and jovial person, he felt out of place in the glossy and ostentatious social milieu of Bombay.

Jaddan Bai, whom Saigal had met earlier in Calcutta, was a well-known cinema personality and her home in Marine Drive was the favoured meeting place of producers, directors, actors, actresses, singers, lyricists and composers. It was Saigal who first noticed Jaddan Bai's

Saigal and Khurshid as Tansen and Tani in *Tansen*

singing talents, her prodigious classical training and her melodious voice. It is likely that his nostalgia for Punjab might have taken him there. Another person close to Saigal was the actor K.N. Singh who was also groomed at New Theatres by Debaki Bose and who had done supporting roles in *Sunehra Sansar* and *Vidyapati* before coming to Bombay in 1937.

The year 1942 also saw another masterpiece from Bombay Talkies, *Basant*, which scored a diamond jubilee run. Directed by Amiya Chakrabarty, it dealt with the drama of a poor girl becoming a star, and brought great fame and fortune to the leading star Mumtaz Shanti, a new find from Lahore.

The famous *Tansen* was the second Saigal film brought out by Ranjit Studios. Directed by Jayant Desai with music by Khemchand Prakash, it was a terrific success with unforgettable songs by both Saigal and his heroine, Khurshid. A love fantasy associated with the life of Tansen, the great musician and one of the *navratna* (nine gems) of Akbar's court, it is still remembered for its songs by the duo, like *Diya jalao* and *Barso*

With Khurshid in *Tansen*

re, representing the Deepak and Malhar ragas; one is believed to light up lamps and the other to bring showers of rain.

Tansen was easily Saigal's best-known film from Bombay. It was the greatest musical in its time, with thirteen songs written by the two leading lyricists, D.N. Madhok and Pandit Indra. Saigal's striking duet with Khurshid, *More bala pan ke sath*, reminded listeners of Saigal's duets with Kanan Bala in *Street Singer*. Khurshid's performance in *Tansen* was recognized as the best of her career; Saigal undoubtedly contributed to bringing out her best. The powerful impact of Tansen's music is depicted by its taming of a mad elephant, turning a desolate field into a flower garden, and instruments playing on their own to accompany his singing of dhrupad in the royal court.

With Mubarak as Akbar in *Tansen*

The film, directed with admirable skill and insight, shows not only the musical genius that Tansen was but also the legends and anecdotes spun around him during the last 400 years. The most unusual feature of the film was its opening scene, showing the balding and bespectacled Saigal, sitting on a chair in the studio surrounded by camera equipment. He reads out an introduction to the film and explains the need to combine the historical part of Tansen's story with some fictional episodes in order to portray the great musician as a gentle human being with feelings and emotions. He points out that the original story was enriched with some new elements in order to make it interesting for the viewers and he expected them to appreciate the scriptwriter's creative license and watch the film in that spirit.

Saigal's third film under the Ranjit banner was *Bhanwara*, directed by Kidar Sharma, who had by now earned both name and fame as a writer, director, lyricist and producer. Kidar Sharma's association with Saigal went back to his *Devdas* days and he was indebted to Saigal for having introduced him to B.N. Sircar. Sharma was groomed as a filmmaker under the guidance of stalwarts of the New Theatres like Debaki Bose, P.C. Barua and Nitin Bose.

Bhanwara was more or less a failure at the box office. However, Saigal with the playback singer Amir Bai did full justice to the lyrics

With Khurshid in *Tansen*

penned by Kidar Sharma with music composed by Khemchand Prakash. A lovely duet by the duo *Kya hum ne bigada hai, kyon hum ko satate ho* and some solos by Saigal, such as *Hum apna unhain bana na sake* and *Muskrate hue yun ankh* became popular with Saigal fans, even without their viewing the film.

Now that Saigal had joined the tribe of freelance stars with no commitment to any particular studio or filmmaker, there was a virtual flood of offers from both established as well as new producers. Saigal had returned from Calcutta after completing *My Sister* in 1944. It was a popular hit but the record-breaking film of the year was *Rattan* directed by M. Sadiq with Swaranlata and Karan Dewan in the leading roles. It was Naushad's music and Zohra Bai Agrewali's melodious songs that contributed to its immense popularity.

Saigal accepted an offer from Jayant Desai, the director of *Tansen*, who had set up his own production unit, Jupiter Studio. Desai had been a well-known front-line Ranjit director for more than a decade and had won acclaim for his devotionals and historicals like *Sant Tulsidas* and *Samrat Chandragupta*. He was anxious to cast a singer–actress opposite the legendary Saigal after the dismal fate of *Bhanwara*. The only singing actresses in Bombay at the time (1945) were Noor Jehan and Suraiya, both much in demand.

Saigal with Sohrab Modi at Minerva Studio, Bombay

After her arrival from Lahore, Noor Jehan—with her beauty and voice—was fast climbing the ladder of name and fame. She had already created a sensation with her performance in *Zeenat*, a fantastic box-office hit. But Desai, having cast Suraiya in his latest film *Chandragupta*, chose her to co-star with Saigal in his planned production *Tadbir* under his own banner. The first Saigal–Suraiya musical was created around a story about destiny and against fatalism. Suraiya did justice to her role and in addition to delightful duets with Saigal like *Rani khol de apne dwar milne ka din ah gaya*, she also sang solo numbers to supplement

With Suraiya in *Parwana*

In *Parwana*

In *Parwana*

Saigal's enchanting songs like *Janam janam ka dukhia prani* and *Main kismat ka mara*. The film was not a box-office hit but had a modicum of success.

For the first time, Saigal's failing health came to be noticed though his golden voice was intact. Yet Bombay producers raced to book Saigal for their productions, and to exploit his name and fame as the superstar of the film world.

On his part, Saigal was used to the way of working in the New Theatres where he was expected to work in one or two films a year and that, too, in the same studio. Within a year, Saigal agreed to work in four films. *Kurukshetra*, produced by Unity Productions, Calcutta, was also released in 1945 and went unnoticed. It is remembered only for that popular Saigal number, *Kidhar hai tu ai men tamana*. The second film *Omar Khayyam*, in which Saigal co-starred with Suraiya, made no mark whatsoever. The music directors in Bombay were vying with one another to compose music for Saigal. Finally, it was Naushad who teamed up with Saigal in Kardar's masterpiece *Shah Jehan,* the great musical hit that keeps the memory of Saigal alive with the sublime songs *Gham diya*

Singing *Ai dil-e-bekarar jhoom* in *Shah Jehan*

mustaqil and *Jab dil hi toot gaya*. *Shah Jehan* was released in late 1946 when Saigal was almost bedridden and in a very poor state of health. Earlier, he had also acted in J.K. Nanda's *Parwana*, again with Suraiya. In an interview, Nanda recalled that Saigal was already simultaneously acting in three or four films and it was a great strain on him in his ailing condition. Nanda was apprehensive about the completion of his *Parwana* but Saigal reportedly told him, 'Come what may, I am very confident that I shall complete the entire work of your film. If the time comes, I shall tell even death to wait for a while but shall not cause any interruption to your work. I shall die only after completing my work in the film.'

Saigal's output in Bombay did not compare favourably with his remarkable achievements in New Theatres in Calcutta. The Bombay film world had been dubbed a bazaar by P.C. Barua, the renowned creater of *Devdas*. The Bombay producers did not have directors of the calibre to match stalwarts like Debaki Bose, P.C. Barua and Nitin Bose. Nor did they have accomplished maestros of music like R.C. Boral and Pankaj Mullick who scored music for Saigal. *Tansen* was the only one out of seven films that Saigal made in Bombay which kept his fame and

With Nasreen in *Shah Jehan*

In *Parwana*

popularity, thanks to the music director, Khemchand Prakash, who had inherited the art from his own father, the court singer of Jaipur. He was to earn all-India fame later with his music in *Mahal* in 1949 with the enduring *Ayega aane wala*.

By the beginning of December 1946, Saigal's health deteriored further. He had chronic diabetes. His long-time friend Dr Latif attended to him on the sets while shooting progressed. But Saigal could not bear the strain of shooting, would often stumble on the sets and had to be given medical aid to prop him up.

He hoped against hope that, as in the old Punjabi saying, a change of place and water would improve his health. He left for his home town, Jullundur, on 25 December 1946, hoping to recoup his health after completing all his film commitments.

But he never recovered; he died on the morning of 18 January 1947.

At no stage in his lifetime did Saigal speak about or refer to his film songs. There was a story doing the rounds in the film world that he had wanted *Jab dil hi toot gaya* to be played at his funeral. This is baseless— as confirmed by Saigal's wife Asharani's sister. No band is ever played in Punjab at the cremation of a young person and Saigal was only forty-two when he passed away.

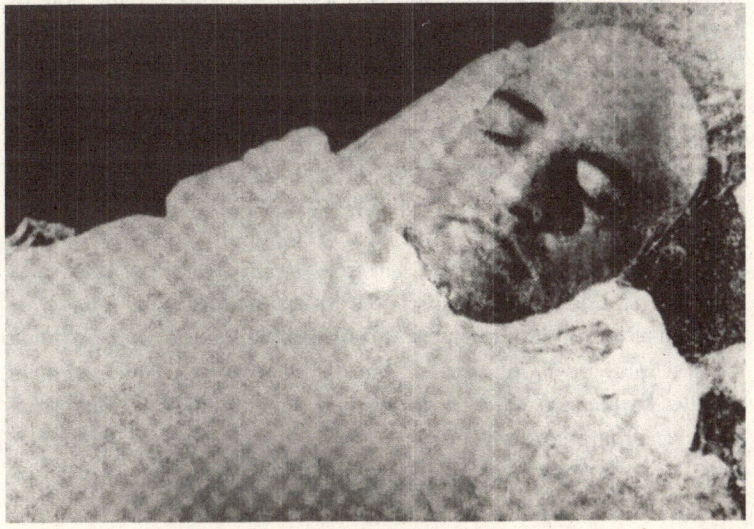

The last journey—18 January 1947

Saigal's Legacy

The founding father of Indian film music, K.L. Saigal was also the last luminary of the gramophone era. His very first record *Jhulana jhulavo* had created history by selling over 5,00,000 copies. Saigal's foremost legacy is the introduction and popularizing of film songs to the Indian public. Until his appearance on the music scene, film songs, largely lifted from the stage dramas, had a limited appeal and were not even released on gramophone records.

In the early 1930s, after the advent of the talkies, the gramophone company HMV did not consider it viable to produce records of film songs. Then the leading film producer, Madan Theatres, exploited the innovation of sound and converted its popular theatrical stage dramas into films. The themes were mainly stories from mythology and famous Persian love tales like *Shirin Farhad, Laila Majnu, Inder Sabha, Raja Harishchandra, Shakuntala* and *Bilwa Mangal*. Madan's leading singing stars Master Nissar and Miss Kajjan could not make much impact on the music lovers and soon faded away. Other singer–actors with theatrical backgrounds suffered similar fates. The talkies brought in a change in people's tastes and they now sought more melodious songs.

K.L. Saigal had already established his reputation as a gramophone celebrity and his songs in New Theatres' *Puran Bhakt* in 1933 were a great hit, heralding the dawn of a new era in film music. His songs were destined to attain the supreme status of 'people's music' in the coming years. It was Saigal's all-time great hit *Balam ayo baso mere man mein* in *Devdas* which created a sensation and Saigal became a national icon. This even prompted New Theatres to release gramophone records of film songs under its own label. Thereafter, Saigal's each and every song was separately recorded and had unprecedented sales all over the country. HMV, which had earlier ignored film songs, now recognized the growing demand for them and began recording every film song, even producing records of earlier popular hits.

K.L. Saigal therefore could rightfully be acclaimed as the architect of this new market for film music records which benefited his contemporary singer–actors, including K.C. Dey, Pahari Sanyal, Kanan Bala, Surendra Nath and Shanta Apte, as well.

Saigal became a legend and a household name in his lifetime. Every other singer–actor of his time tried to emulate him but could not touch him. He is the only singer–actor to have bequeathed to us a treasury of non-film music of bhajans and ghazals. He has inspired both amateur and professional singers of subsequent generations to take to ghazal singing. Saigal selected and composed the ghazals and contributed in no small way to bringing name and fame to forgotten poets whose verses he sang.

Saigal's legacy is most evident in his choice of Ghalib's ghazals, which continue to be favourites for every ghazal singer. Ghazal queen Begum Akhtar observed that no other singer who sang Ghalib ever equalled K.L. Saigal, an estimation supported by many other eminent artistes, including Malika-e-Tarannum Noor Jahan and Iqbal Bano.

The playback era in film music gathered strength only after the demise of Saigal. The next generation of playback singers, including C.H. Atma, Mukesh, Talat Mehmood, Mohammad Rafi and Kishore Kumar, were deeply influenced by Saigal's singing style and struggled to model themselves after him. For them Saigal was an institution in himself and a role model for every aspiring singer. C.H. Atma had been from his childhood a devotee of Saigal and the songs he had sung during his brief career had a flavour of Saigal's style, apparent in his very first record *Pritam aan milo*, recorded in 1945. His film song *Ro-oon mein sagar ke kinare* recorded after Saigal's demise also echoed Saigal's expression. Similarly, Mukesh's first hit song *Dil jalta hai to jalne de* in *Pehli Nazar*, set to music by Anil Biswas, reminded one of Saigal's diction and playing with words. In fact Biswas had worked on Mukesh for a long time, trying to evoke the pathos and pain characteristic of Saigal, whom Mukesh had idolized from his childhood. Talat Mehmood also candidly admitted that it was the ghazal king Saigal who inspired him to take to ghazal singing. His first recorded song *Sab dil ek samaan nahi* is reminiscent of Saigal.

Mohammad Rafi, who got his first break by singing a few lines in chorus in the film *Shah Jehan*, remembered with pride his association with Saigal who had inspired him throughout his career. Kishore Kumar, who had struggled for nearly twenty years before he emerged as a successful playback singer, was a fanatic fan and follower of Saigal. The jester that he was in his boyhood, he would sing for his friends and charge 1 anna for each song, but when he was asked to sing Saigal's songs, he demanded 4 annas for a song. When Kishore was given his first break in the film *Ziddi* he sang *Marne ki duaein kyon maangoon*, copying Saigal's style. Even Saigal's contemporary Surendra Nath, who made his debut in the 1936 film *Deccan Queen*, tried to emulate Saigal. This is evident when one listens to his vintage song *Yaad na kar dil-e-hazin*.

It was difficult for the singers of the 1950s to break away from Saigal's spell. Saigal's persona and voice had gripped the nation and even renowned music directors and maestros of classical music were amazed at Saigal's spontaneous response to words and sounds based on traditional ragas. Such was the allure of Saigal's voice that even the ordinary man felt as if he himself was singing. Melody composers were also influenced by Saigal's manner of rendering songs. The first generation of song writers, including Kidar Sharma, Shailendra, Pandit Indra and D.N. Madhok, were greatly influenced by Saigal's diction and expression and his inimitable way of playing with words.

Saigal set such high standards that they are nearly impossible to improve upon. Many singers tried to imitate him but Saigal's clones did not last long. In fact music directors had to advise even talented playback singers to avoid apeing Saigal and evolve their own style.

Saigal's influence is also evident in more recent ghazal singers, including Jagjit Singh, Mehdi Hasan, Amanat Ali, Salim Raza and Ghulam Ali. With Saigal as their role model, these non-film personalities moulded their own styles, which appealed to listeners even when they sang numbers Saigal had already sung. In the post-Saigal period there are technical innovations, sophisticated means of recording voices and the introduction of several new music instruments.

K.L. Saigal has been the only singer in the world to be heard at a particular time-slot—7.57 a.m. to 8.00 a.m. on Radio Ceylon for over fifty years. During the mid-1950s, Vijay Kishore Dubey introduced a programme of old hit songs in the morning when the radio started its

Hindi service under his supervision. He hailed Saigal's voice as the voice of the century on the subcontinent and decided to have one of Saigal's songs at the end of the daily programme. The practice has continued since.

The magic of legends like Saigal never withers. He has been acclaimed as a Tansen of the modern period, who even surpassed Emperor Akbar's royal singer in popularity—Akbar's Tansen enchanted the Mughal ruling elite and nobility and was not accessible to the masses.

As a mark of honour to Saigal, his birth centenary celebrations were organized at various centres in India in 2004. There are several Saigal memorial societies in India and in many centres in the UK and the US. They hold regular functions on K.L. Saigal's birth and death anniversaries where tributes are paid to the immortal singer. Young singers are invited to these functions to pay a musical homage by singing popular Saigal songs. The performances of the singers are evaluated by the connoisseurs of music and Saigal fans and awards and prizes are distributed. Newspapers, magazines and some TV channels on their part publish pictorial features on Saigal and broadcast special programmes devoted to Saigal's films and songs. At a special programme organized a few years ago by the Environment Society of India at Chandigarh, the youngest child to participate was a three-year-old Sayen Dey, who won a prize amidst thunderous applause, and an audio-cassette of Bengali songs was released through him.

Saigal's recorded music continues to have a ready market in the subcontinent and abroad. Beginning with 78 rpm records, Saigal's songs continue to be released along with the development in recording technology, first in extended play form (45 rpm) followed by the LP records (33 rpm) and cassettes and now they are available in CDs.

Several eminent singers, including Ashok Khosla, Sudesh Bhosle and Dr Ravi Wankhede, have paid their *shraddhanjali* to Saigal by singing his popular hits. Melody queen Lata Mangeshkar paid her tribute by singing the following songs: *So jaa rajkumari*; *Mein kya janoon kya jadoo hai*; *Nainheen ko raah dikha prabhu*; *Balam ayo baso*; *Do naina matware*; *Ab mein kaah karoon kith jaoon*; and *Sat suran teen gram*.

There are several sites on the internet dedicated to Saigal and there is even a site where Saigal's songs are discussed and information about the availability of his films and rare songs exchanged. Given below are the names of a few sites which should be of interest to readers:

http://www.upperstall.com/people/klsaigal.html
http://members.tripod.com/oldies_club/klsaigal.htm
http://www.sawf.org/audio/shankara/klsaigal.ram
http://www.sampurna.sdnpk.org/images/KLSaigal.doc

To conclude, I quote Babu Rao Patel, legendary editor of *Filmindia* who observed, 'People didn't merely love Saigal, they revered his glorious voice and called it divine. Saigal tuned music into a simple emotional poetry of the soul—he can't be forgotten so easily, not till this music-mad nation suddenly goes deaf.'

I would also like to quote eminent music director Naushad's poetic tribute to Saigal:

Mere dil ko yakin hai ye mukammal,
Naghmon ki kasam aaj bhi zinda hai wo Saigal,
Saigal ko faramosh koi kar nahi sakta,
Wo aisa amar hai ke kabhi mar nahi sakta

(Naushad proclaims with complete confidence that Saigal is very much alive; no one can ignore or forget him as he is among those who defy death and are immortal).

Appendix A
Tribute by *Filmindia*—
February 1947

Saigal—The Man Who Thrilled a Nation?

Born on 14 April 1904 at Jammu, Kundal Lal Saigal took the country by storm with his thrilling and melodious voice. Never before had the Indian screen presented such a glorious singer with so much of emotion and pathos in his music. With millions in the country, *Filmindia* mourns the passing of an incomparable artiste. The artiste has gone but his unique melody is with us in innumerable records and films—a proud heritage of a music-mad nation.

For a week, after the daily papers flashed the news of Saigal's death, riots, politics and Pakistan went out of news and the Hindus, the Muslims, the Christians, the Jews, the touchables and the untouchables—one and all reverently discussed the sad and sudden death of Kundan Lal Saigal, the greatest singer the Indian screen had ever produced in its long history of misadventure.

People didn't merely love Saigal. They revered his glorious voice and called it divine. In his death died the music of millions of souls and it was no wonder to find every person, with a musical ear, a mourner with millions of music lovers all over the country.

Trains, buses, trams, taxis, streets, theatres, parks, the racecourse—wherever one happened to be it was the dead Saigal that lived again in the memory of his affectionate fans. Men and women, boys and girls, the young and the old, the rich and the poor—one and

133

all told one another what a great singer Saigal had been and each according to the mould of his mind quoted a different song as the greatest memory of the dead artiste.

Saigal was the one single person who had given the screen music a rare emotion which soothed the aching souls of people in the travails of modern life.

Millions wept with him when in *Devdas* his unforgettable song: *Sukh ke din ab beetat nahin* came from the screen with its agonizing melody and yet in its very agony gave to the millions rare soothe, for in Saigal's rare voice there was pathos and joy, pain and pleasure, a stab and a soothe all at once wedded to an incomparable melody never before heard on the screen anywhere in the world. Saigal was easily the world's most emotional male singer.

Built an Industry

Saigal took the screen music into every home in the country and in doing so lent to the Indian film industry a stability which a hundred of its so-called industrial captains would have failed to give in another hundred years.

'Singing like Saigal' became a national proverb and proud parents often introduced their progeny in society with this proverb and proceeded to prove their claim by asking the child to sing a Saigal song.

Saigal turned music into a simple emotional poetry of the soul. People only needed a voice, a little ear for music, and the emotion to sing a Saigal song. The mathematics of music vomitted by the bearded and roaring gorilla of the country were hardly needed for Saigal's soulful music, which seemed to come directly from the heart and was intended to go directly to the heart of the listener.

Is Saigal dead? The man is no more but his music will live. Over a million records of Saigal's songs must be playing at this very moment in a million homes all over the country.

When he lived, Saigal sang and lulled a nation into an emotional coma but now after his death he will haunt a nation with his inimitable voice. From every home will come the dead man's glorious voice, intruding on the neighbours, reminding one and all that though this man died like all mortals, his music still lives. Saigal can't be forgotten so easily, not till this music-mad nation suddenly goes dead and ceases to hypnotize itself with the soulful melodies which the great artiste has left behind as a precious heritage for posterity.

His Democratic Melody

Today it is considered a great art to imitate Saigal and some of those who imitate him sometimes fancy themselves as better musicians than Saigal. These snobs may some day forget Saigal but there will still be thousands of half-naked beggars in the streets of India, little boys who sing Saigal's songs and induce the people to give them a few coppers to buy their evening meal. Saigal's songs have not only helped the rich to while their idle hours away but they have also provided the wherewithal to thousands of needy ones to earn their daily livelihood. Saigal's music was a democratic fare which both the rich and the poor enjoyed with the same relish.

Kundan Lal Saigal was born at Jammu on 11 April 1904 in a middle-class family. His parents thought that Saigal's elder brother had talent for music and a teacher was kept to teach him music.

While his brother was taught, Saigal heard and learnt without even meaning to do so. Nature's harp was inside him and unconsciously the old music teacher played on its strings giving Saigal a realization of his own musical talent.

After a common and uninteresting career in school, Saigal ultimately became a clerk on the North Western Railway. A few years later he was on the move sometimes as a typist, as a salesman or as a hotel manager.

Twelve years ago, he landed in Calcutta and managed to contact Mr B.N. Sircar, the New Theatres' Chief. It was a love-at-first-sight friendship between the two, which lasted till the last day of Saigal in this world.

It was with rare judgment that Mr Sircar decided the future brilliant career of Saigal on the screen. With his face and figure against him, very few producers would have risked money merely on a man's voice. In fact in an earlier attempt which Saigal had made in Bombay to secure an acting role, a leading producer had flatly refused to consider even his voice for playback music.

But Sircar, the sentimental Bengali intellectual, knew the music-mad people of his country and like a shrewd businessman he also realized that in the glorious voice of Saigal there was a goldmine hidden for a film producer.

Saigal Arrives

Saigal was soon cast in a picture for grooming. His first picture was *Zinda Lash* but he wasn't noticed till in *Chandidas*, he sang those pathetic lines *Tarapat beete din raen*. The natural pathos in his voice intruded on the people and disturbed their emotions all right but Umashashi attracted more attention and Saigal did not ultimately arrive though 'Chandidas' scored a huge success at the box-offices. 'Chandidas' made Uma Shashi a star.

It was when *Devdas* was released that Saigal's golden voice touched the tender chords in a million hearts. The very first song *Balam aaye baso more man mein* was received with such terrific approval by the crowds that in the pathetic part of the picture where Saigal sang his famous song *Sukh ke din ab beetat nahin,* the crowds didn't have to squeeze their hearts much to shed tears in sympathy with their hero.

Even before the show of *Devdas* ended, Saigal had arrived. He was a star now. From *Devdas* onwards millions all over India, in towns and villages, rushed to see and hear Saigal often without knowing even the name of the picture he worked in. To millions Saigal's very name meant a guarantee of almost divine melody.

Sircar, the shrewd Bengali producer, gave full scope to Saigal's remarkable talent. Pictures after pictures starring Saigal came to the screen one after another. *Dharti Mata, Daku Mansoor, President, Karwan-e-Hayat, Dushman, Zindagi, Lagan, Street Singer, Krorepati, My Sister* and many others—one and all dragged millions out of their homes to the rotten Indian theatres to hear the magic notes of a golden voice. Saigal's spell was irresistible and New Theatres made several fortunes—not merely one.

Money Talks

At this stage gold gave a new shape to Saigal's destiny. Tempted by money he came to Bombay to work in Ranjit and other studios. He did quite a few pictures in Bombay: *Bhakt Surdas, Tansen, Bhanwara, Shah Jehan, Tadbir, Omar Khayyam*, but not in one of them could be heard the old magic of Saigal's golden voice. Gold had taken the golden out of his voice in this city where the smoke coming out of the mill-chimneys smells of human souls.

In his very first picture in Bombay, Saigal's music died without even a struggle. The Bombay producers seemed to throttle the great artiste and squeeze the soul out of his throat. They fed the body but murdered the spirit.

Saigal's last picture was *Parwana* which is still in the editing room.

Affable, affectionate and smiling, Saigal was a model of gentleness. An ailing man for years, he lived on his own optimism till the last day of his life. His was a world of friends, for his melody instantly dissolved any possible differences he would have had with his fellow human beings.

Saigal's only bitter experience was one regrettable incident which comedian Dixit reports. Saigal once expressed a desire to meet producer-director V. Shantaram and encouraged by Dixit accompanied him to the Rajkamal Kalamandir to pay his respects to the director whose film craftsmanship Saigal had often admired.

A word was sent to the great director of Saigal's desire to meet him but the great man had no time. He was too busy with his rehearsals.

Saigal went back a wiser man perhaps to sing another sad song of life—a song that may still bring tears to a million eyes.

Saigal was a bard who sang the poetic sighs of the human soul and warmed the heart of a heartless world. May his soul rest in peace. Amen!

1932

Mohabbat ke Aansoo

Producer: The New Theatres Ltd, Calcutta
Director: P. Atorthy
Music: R.C. Boral
Cast: K.L. Saigal, Akhtari Muradabadi, Sadiq Ansari, Mahajabeen

1932

Zinda Lash

Producer: The New Theatres Ltd, Calcutta
Director: P. Atorthy
Music: R.C. Boral
Cast: K.L. Saigal, Hafizjee, Ansari, Siddiqui, Mahajabeen, Rani, Ali Mir, Kapur, Hamid

1932

Subah ka Sitara

Producer: The New Theatres Ltd, Calcutta
Director: Nitin Bose
Music: R.C. Boral
Cast: K.L. Saigal, Ratnabai, Siddiqui, Ansari, Ali Mir, Mazhar Khan

1933

Puran Bhakt

Producer: The New Theatres Ltd, Calcutta
Director: Debaki Bose
Music: R.C. Boral
Cast: Kumar, Anwari, K.C. Dey, Bikram Kapoor, Tara,
           Uma Shashi, K.L. Saigal, Siddiqui, Ansari

1933

Rajrani Meera

Producer: The New Theatres Ltd, Calcutta
Director: Debaki Bose
Music: R.C. Boral
Cast: Durga Khote, Prithviraj Kapoor, Pahari Sanyal,
           K.L. Saigal, Molina, Ansari, Siddiqui, Indubala,
           Rattan Bai, Indra Mohan Surma

1933

Yahoodi Ki Ladki

Producer: The New Theatres Ltd, Calcutta
Director: P. Atorthy
Music: Pankaj Mullick
Cast: K.L. Saigal, Rattan Bai, Nawab, Kumar, Pahari Sanyal,
           Hamid, Ghulam Mohammad, Radharani, Tara

1933

Dulari Bibi

Producer: The New Theatres Ltd, Calcutta
Director: Debaki Bose
Cast: K.L. Saigal, Molina Devi, Mir Jaan

1934

Chandidas

Producer: The New Theatres Ltd, Calcutta
Director: Nitin Bose
Music: R.C. Boral
Cast: K.L. Saigal, Uma Shashi, Pahari Sanyal, Nawab, M. Ansari,
           I.H. Sadiq, Parbati, Anwari Bai

1934

Daku Mansoor

Producer: The New Theatres Ltd, Calcutta
Director: Nitin Bose
Music: R.C. Boral
Cast: Prithviraj Kapoor, Husn Banu, Uma Shashi, K.L. Saigal,
           Pahari Sanyal, Nemo

1934

Mohabbat ki Kasauti (Rooplekha)

Producer: The New Theatres Ltd, Calcutta
Director: P.C. Barua
Music: R.C. Boral
Cast: Ratnabai, Pahari Sanyal, Vishwanath, Noor Mohammad,
           K.L. Saigal

1935

Karwan-e-Hayat

Producer: The New Theatres Ltd, Calcutta
Director: P. Atorthy
Music: R.C. Boral
Cast: K.L. Saigal, Rajkumari, Pahari Sanyal, Molina Shyama
           Zutshi, Nawab, Rattan Bai, Siddiqui, Kapoor

1935

Debdaas (in Bangla)

Producer: The New Theatres Ltd, Calcutta
Director: P.C. Barua
Music: R.C. Boral
Cast: P.C. Barua, Jamuna, K.L. Saigal, K.C. Dey, Prabhabati, Amar Mullick

1935

Devdas

Producer: The New Theatres Ltd, Calcutta
Director: P.C. Barua
Music: Timir Baran
Cast: K.L. Saigal, Jamuna, Rajkumar, A.H. Shore, Nemo, P.C. Barua, K.C. Dey, B. Bahaduri, Pahari Sanyal, Sitara, Kidar Sharma, Bikram Kapoor

1936

Bijoya (in Bangla)

Producer: The New Theatres Ltd, Calcutta
Director: Dinesh Ranjan Dass
Music: Timir Baran
Cast: Pahari Sanyal, Chandrabati, K.L. Saigal, K.C. Dey, Amar Mullick

1936

Crorepati (Millionaire)

Producer: The New Theatres Ltd, Calcutta
Director: Hem Chunder
Music: R.C. Boral, Pankaj Mullick
Cast: Molina, K.L. Saigal, Trilok Kapoor, Pahari Sanyal,

Nawab, Jagdish, Babulal, Rajkumari, Kidar Sharma,
Devbala, Amar Mullick, Nemo, Sardar Akhtar

1936

Devdaasaa (The Tamil Version of Devdas)

Producer: The New Theatres Ltd, Calcutta
Director: P.V. Rao
Cast: P.V. Rao (as Devdas) T.S. Krishna Iyengar, T.M. Ramasamy
          Pillai, K.L. Saigal, S.N. Vijayalakshmi, G.B. Rajayee

1936

Pujarin

Producer: The New Theatres Ltd, Calcutta
Director: Prafulla Roy
Music: Timir Baran
Cast: K.L. Saigal, Chandra, Pahari Sanyal, K.C. Dey, Rajkumari,
          Nawab, Jagdish Sethi

1937

Deedee (in Bangla)

Producer: The New Theatres Ltd, Calcutta
Director: Nitin Bose
Music: R.C. Boral and Pankaj Mullick
Cast: K.L. Saigal, Chandravati, Leela Desai, Durgadas,
          Bandyopadhyaya, Deobala, Amar Mullick

1937

President (Didi)

Producer: The New Theatres Ltd, Calcutta
Director: Nitin Bose
Music: R.C. Boral, Pankaj Mullick

Cast: Kamlesh Kumari, K.L. Saigal, Nawab, Leela Desai,
           Prithviraj Kapoor, Jagdish Sethi, Bikram Kapoor

1938

Desher Maate

Producer: The New Theatres Ltd, Calcutta
Director: Nitin Bose
Music: Pankaj Mullick
Cast: K.L. Saigal, Chandravati, Uma Shashi, K.C. Dey,
           Pankaj Mullick, Durgadas Bandyopadhyaya.

1938

Dharti Mata

Producer: The New Theatres Ltd, Calcutta
Director: Nitin Bose
Music: Pankaj Mullick
Cast: K.L. Saigal, Jagdish Sethi, Nemo, Kamlesh Kumari, Uma
           Shashi, Nawab, K.C. Dey, Bikram Kapoor, Shyam Laha

1938

Saathee (in Bangla)

Producer: The New Theatres Ltd, Calcutta
Director: Phani Mazumdar
Music: R.C. Boral
Cast: K.L. Saigal, Kanan Devi, Amar Mullick, Kamla Jharia,
           Sailen Chowdhury

1938

Street Singer

Producer: The New Theatres Ltd, Calcutta
Director: Phani Mazumdar

Music: R.C. Boral
Cast: K.L. Saigal, Kanan Devi, Jagdish Sethi, Bikram Kapoor

1939

Dushman (Jiban Maran)

Producer: The New Theatres Ltd, Calcutta
Director: Nitin Bose
Music: Pankaj Mullick
Cast: K.L. Saigal, Leela Desai, Najmul, Prithviraj Kapoor, Nemo,
        Deobala, Manorama, Jagdish Sethi, Bikram Kapoor

1939

Jeeban Maran

Producer: The New Theatres Ltd, Calcutta
Director: Nitin Bose
Music: Pankaj Mullick
Cast: K.L. Saigal, Leela Desai, Bhanu Bandyopadhyaya,
        Amar Mullick

1940

Zindagi

Producer: The New Theatres Ltd, Calcutta
Director: P.C. Barua
Music: Pankaj Mullick
Cast: K.L. Saigal, Jamuna, Pahari Sanyal, Nemo, Ashalata,
        Shyam Laha, Sitara, Bikram Kapoor, Manorama

1941

Lagan (Parichay)

Producer: The New Theatres Ltd, Calcutta
Director: Nitin Bose

Music: Pankaj Mullick
Cast: K.L. Saigal, Kanan Devi, Jagdish Sethi, Nawab,
            Nemo, G. Vaid

1941

Parichoy (in Bangla)

Producer: The New Theatres Ltd, Calcutta
Director: Nitin Bose
Music: R.C. Boral
Cast: K.L. Saigal, Kanan Devi, Ratin Bandyopadhyaya,
            Mihir Bhattacharya

1942

Bhakt Surdas

Producer: Shree Ranjit Movietone Company Ltd
Director: Chaturbhuj Doshi
Music: Gyan Dutt
Cast: K.L. Saigal, Khurshid, Monica Desai, Nagendra,
            M. Saigal, N. Desai, Gharpure, Kesarbai, B. Sharma,
            Bashir

1943

Tansen

Producer: Shree Ranjit Movietone Company Ltd
Director: Jayant Desai
Music: Khemchand Prakash
Cast: K.L. Saigal, Khurshid, Mubarak, Nagendra, Kamala
            Chatterji, Kesari, Bhagwandas

1944

Bhanwara

Producer: Shree Ranjit Movietone Company Ltd

Director: Kidar Sharma
Music: Khemchand Prakash
Cast: K.L. Saigal, Aroon, Kamala Chatterji, Monica Desai,
            Yakub, Brijmala

1944

Meri Bahen (My Sister)

Producer: The New Theatres Ltd
Director: Hem Chunder
Music: Pankaj Mullick
Cast: K.L. Saigal, Sumitra Devi, Nawab, Akhtar Jehan,
            Chandravati, Hiralal, Tulsi Chakravarty, Tandon,
            Shore, Rajlaxmi

1945

Kurukshetra

Producer: Unity Productions
Director: R. Sharma
Music: Ganpatrao
Cast: K.L. Saigal, Nawab, Hanti, Udvadia, Mohammad, Biman,
            Banerji, Radharani

1945

Tadbir

Producer: Jayant Desai Productions
Director: Jayant Desai
Music: Lal Mohammad
Cast: K.L. Saigal, Suraiya, Mubarak, Jiloo, Salvi, Rehana,
            Ravishankar, Shashi Kapoor

1946

Omar Khayyam

Producer: Murari Productions

Director: Mohan Sinha
Music: Lal Mohammad
Cast: K.L. Saigal, Suraiya, Wasti, Benjamin, Shakir, Leela,
            Madan Puri, Mazzammil

1946

Shah Jehan

Producer: Kardar Productions
Director: A.R. Kardar
Music: Naushad
Cast: K.L. Saigal, Ragini, Jairaj, Nasreen, Himalaya,
            Sulochana Chatterji, Azurie, Anwari, Rehman

1947

Parwana

Producer: Jeet Productions
Director: J.K. Nanda
Music: Khurshid Anwar
Cast: K.L. Saigal, Suraiya, S. Nazir, Najma, K.N. Singh, Azurie

Appendix C

I

Memorable Songs
Author's Selection for HMV LPs, 1965

Song 1

Main baithi thi phulwari mein
Ek sakhi aa gayee aur boli
Kya soch hai tumko bolo to
Hun behan tumhari munhboli

Kuchh kah na saki
Munh takat rahi
Nainon se chali ansuvan toli
Chalte chalte vohi bol gayee
Sakhi kaun des raaje piyara

Vo sunte hi khamosh hui
Aur nain bhaye bauraan sakhi
Main chaha usko chet karun
Tha jaane usko maan sakhi

Jab hosh hui tab kahne lagi
Yehi tha mujhko bhi dhyaan sakhi
Aur yehi main kahne wali thi
Kaun des raaje piyara

Kuchh na samjhi kya kahe sakhi
Bin jaane dhoondhan chal nikli
Jangal upvan tribhuvan dhoondha
Par kahin na uski ter mili
Aakhir thak kar main baith gayee
Aur lagi poochne kaho koi
Sundar chhabi jiski kahte hain
Vo kaun des raje piyara

Tab man ne meethi baat kahi
Kyoon tune itni baat gahi
Ghar baithe pi pa sakti thi
Main bidhi bataun vo kya thi
Bahar ke naina moond sakhi
Aur nain hriday ke khol sakhi
Ab apane munh se bol sakhi
Sakhi kaun des raaje piyara

—Written by K.L. Saigal

Song 2

Hamjoliyon ki thi toliyaan
Vo kar rahi thi thitholiyaan
Kuchh mast thi sangeet mein
Kuchh khelti thi holiyan

Ik main hoon dukhiya janamjali
Gham mein huee gham mein pali
Gham hi mera hamraaz tha
Gham hi ki thi deeksha mili

Chaha ke main bhi ik zara
Dekhun ke aakhir hai ye kya
Kyoon khush hain saari ladkiyaan
Paya hai kya khoya hua

Dekha to sacchi baat thi
Sab ki suhaag ki raat thi

Apne piya ko saath Ie
Dale vo haath mein haath thi

Masti mein thin sab jhoomti
Apne piya ko choomtin
Kabhi dekh drishti se prem ki
Anand lekar jhoomtin

Kamatr sab vo ho gayin
Khamosh hokar so gayin
Jis ka piya tha saath tha
Madhosh hokar kho gayin

Main hoon mera na hai piya
Tadpe hamesha hai jiya
Dekha kisi ko dekh kar
Behla liya apna jiya

Bhagvan kare aisa na ho
Dukh ho magar aisa na ho
Jis se piya bairaag ho
Aisa na ho aisa na ho

—Written by K. L. Saigal

Song 3

Suno suno hey Krishan kala
Aaee tumre dwaar suno meri pukar
Ab sun le baansari wala
Suno suno he Krishan kala

Tum jante hue jo na jano naath
Ab kahsey kahoon dukh sara—suno
Mere paon to hon aur main aa na sakun
Hoon adheen main he dinanath
Jo main chhal se aaun kahoon
Jale aaun to log karen badnaam

Jaisi jo chahe baatain udaye
Kahe radha bhi mohe kalankini
Tose chori jo milne aaye
Jaisi chahai jo batain udahai
Main to bol sakun
Munh na khol sakun
Prabhu jab hi to abla naam
Mora jeevan jaaye na daras dikhaye
Na dikhaye daras ghanshyam
Na dikhaye daras mope dekho sakhi
Nahin khaye taras
More man ki rahi man mein haye
Haye more nainan ne
Dekha nahin abhi shyam
Abla ka dukh he dinanath
Man ki rahe hai man mein
Chandidas kahe sakhi hai, sakhi hai
Chandidas kahe jis tan lage
Wohi tan ye dukhda jane

Song 4

Kaun bujhave ho ram tapat more man ki ho rama
Laagi aag lagan ki hai ram-rama ho ram
Kaun bujhave tapat more manki rama
Preetam gaya videsh sakhi
Kaho kaase kahun man ki batiyaan
Birha agan phoonkyo man mora
Ab kaun kare sheetal chhatiyaan Rama kaun bujhave

Song 5

Bhajun main to bhav se Siri Giridhari
Hriday mein ab dhun hai krishn nam ki nyari
Mithya hai mamta mithya hai hamta
Mithya sakal sansari
Bhav bhaye bhanjan jan man ranjan
Sakal kasht do taari

Hriday mein ab dhun hai
Krishn naam ki nyari
Bhog vilaas paya chahoon na dil se
Krishn ka naam ik bhaaya
Krishn hi krishn hai man ke andar
Dou charanan mein balihari

Song 6

Kadm chalai aagai man pachhe bhagai
Kaisa hai ye jal moh ka kaise puccai dhagai
Main bisraun wo yad ayain sath sath unkai parchhain
Kaise unsai ankh churayain jin sai naina lagai
     man pachhai
More mandir prabhu tum bas jao man sai chinta moh chhudao
Murli par yehi tair sunavo vahin savera jahan jagai-
     Man pachhe—

Song 7

Nain heen ko rah dikha prabhu
Pag pag thokar khaun main
Tumri nagria ki kathin dagria
Chalat chalat gir jaun main prabhu-Nain
Chahun aur merai ghor andhera
Bhool na jaun dwar tera
Aik bar prabhu haath pakad lo
Man ka deep jalaun main prabhu-Nain

Song 8

Ye kaisa anyaye data, ye kaisa—
Mera banta kaam bigad kar bigdai kaam banaye
Bedha par lagaye data, ye kaisa—
Dukh jhelun jis sukh ke karan
Wo sukh bhi chhin jaye
Jaise apne diye ki jyoti, dujai ke ghar jaye—data

Main bhi yuhin jama rahunga kaisa hi toofan aye
Ghat ka pathar hil nahin sakta
Lakh thepaidain khaye
Kabhi to dukh ko sukh kar dega Anyaee ka nyaye
Andha to jab hi patiyaye jab do anken paye—data

Song 9

Sapt suran teen gram gao sab guni jan
Ikees murchhna ban taan ko milayo
Audav sankeern swar sampuran raag bhed
Alankar bhushan ban raag ko sajao-sapt sur teen
Sa sur sadho man re apnai rab ko jan
Gandhar tajo ghuman madhyam moksh pao
Pancham parmeshwar dhaivat dharo dhyan
Nee jis din prabhu charan chit lagao-sapt sur teen—

Song 10

Avasar beeto jaat praani tero
Avasar beeto jaat
Is kaal ki herapheri mein
Tero avasar beeto jaat
Saath minat guzre gaya ghanta
Chaubis mein din raat
Pal pal karke khinna hot hai
Ik aawat ik jaat
Prani tero avasar beeto jaat
Chhe ritu mil kar varsh hot hai
Ritu ritu mein do maas
Maas maas mein tees diwas hain
Gayee sandhya ayee praat
Prani tero avasar beeto jaat

Balakpan gaya khel kood mein
Jauban yuvati saath
Vridh bhayo kachhu ban nahin aave ?
kaanpat tero haath
Prani tero avasar beeto jaat

Song 11

Bakadr-e-shauq ikraar-e-wafa kya
Hamaare shauq ki hai intaha kya

Dil-e-aafat zada ka mudda kya
Shikasta saaz kya uski sada kya

Muhabbat ka yehi jab shaghal thehra
To phir aah-e-rasa kya na rasa kya

Dua dil se jo nikle kaargar ho
Yahan dil hi nahin dil se dua kya

Salaamat daamn e ummid e 'Seemab'
Muhabbat mein kisi ka aasra kya

—Seemab

Song 12

Ishq khud mailey hijab hai aaj
Husn majbure izterab hai aaj
Nalaye dil ko dil se lag nahin
Nagma azurdaye rubab hai aaj
Maikada gamkada hai terai begair
Sarnagun shish-o-sharab hai aaj
Zindagi jismain sans laiti thee
Wo zamana khyalo khwab hai aaj
Mit gaye dil ke walvalai 'Seemab'
Khatm afsanay-e-shabab hai aaj

—Seemab

Song 13

Phir mujhe dida-e-tar yad aaya
Dil jigar tishna-e-fariyad aaya

Dam liya tha na kayaamat ne hanoz
Ke tera vaqt-e-safar yaad aaya

Koi veerani si veerani hai
Dasht ko dekh ke ghar yaad aaya

Maine Majnoon pe ladakpan mein 'Asad'
Sang uthaya tha ke sar yaad aaya

—Mirza Ghalib

Song 14

Laaee hayat aaye kaza le chali chale
Apni khushi na aaye na apni khushi chale

Behtar to hai yehi ke na duniyan se dil lage
Par kya karein jo kaam na bedillagi chale

Duniya ne kiska rah-e-fana mein diya hai saath
Tum bhi chale chalo yuhin jabtak chali chale

Jaate hawa-e-shauq mein hain is chaman se ai Zauq
Apni bala se baad-e-saba ab kabhi chale

—Zauq

Song 15

Ab kya bataoon main tere milne se kya mila
Irfan e gham hua mujhe dil ka pata mila

Jab door tak na koi fakeer ashna mila
Tera niyazmand tere dar se ja mila

Manzil mili murad mili mudda mila
Sab kuchh mujhe mila jo tera naksh-e-pa mila

Ya zakhm-e-dil ko cheer ke seene se phaink de
ya aitaraaf kar ke nishan-e-wafa mila

'Seemab' ko shagufta na dekha tamam umr
Kambakht jab mila hame gham aashna mila

—Seemab

Song 16

Harek baat pe kahte ho tum ke tu kya hai
Tum hi bataao ye andaaz-e-guftagu kya hai

Ragon mein daudne phirne ke ham nahin kayal
Jab aankh hi se na tapka to vo lahoo kya hai

Piyoon sharaab agar khum bhi dekh loon do chaar
Ye shisha-o-kadah-o kuza o-suboo kya hai

Hua hai shah ka musahib phire hai itrata
Vagarna shahar mein Ghalib ki abroo kya hai

—Mirza Ghalib

Song 17

Main unhain chhedun aur kuchh na kahain
Chal nikaltai jo maiy piye hotai
Kaiher ho za bala ho jo kuchh ho
Kash ke tum merai liye hotai
Meri kismat main gam gar itna tha
Dil bhi ya rab kayi diye hotai
Aa bhi jata ley rah par 'Ghalib'
Koi din aur bhi jiye hotai

—Mirza Ghalib

Song 18

Wo aake khwaab mein taskeen-e-izteraab to de
vale mujhe tapshe-dil majaal e khwaab to de

Kare hai qatl lagawat mein tera ro dena
Teri tarha koi tegh-e-nigaah ko aab to de

Pila de oak se saqi jo hamse nafrat hai
pyala gar nahin deta na de sharaab to de

'Asad' khushi se mere haath paon phool gaye
Kaha jo usne zara mere paon daab to de

—Mirza Ghalib

Song 19

Ek ahley dard ney sunsan jo dekha kafas
Bola ab aati nahin hai kyon sadaye andleeb
Balopar do char dikhlakar kaha saiyad ney
Ze nishani reh gayi hai ab bajaye andleeb

Kaun viraney mein dekhega bahar
Phool jungle mein khiley kin kai liye
Dil ka zaman tu tera kya aitbar
Pehlai ik zaman ho zaman ke liye
Lash par ibrat ze kehti thi 'Ameer'
Aye thai duniya mein is din ke liye

Song 20

Duniya mein hoon duniya ka talabgar nahin hoon
Bazar se guzra hoon khareedar nahin hoon

Zinda hoon magar zeest ki lazzat nahin baqi
Har chand ke hoon hosh mein hoshiyar nahin hoon

Is khana-e-hasti se guzar jayoonga belaus
Saya hoon fakt nakshb-e-deevar nahin hoon

Wo gul hoon khizan ne jise barbaad kiya hai
Uljhoon kisi daaman se main vo khaar nahin hoon

—Akbar Allahabadi

Song 21

Dil se teri nigah jigar tak utar gayi
Donon ko ik ada mein razamand kar gayi

Wo baada-e-shabana ki kharmastiyaan kahan
Uthiye bas ke lazzat-e-khwaab-e-sahar gayi

Dekho to dil farebi-e-andaaz-e-naksh-o-pa
Mauje kheran mein yaar bhi kya gul katar gayi

Nazzare ne bhi kaam kiya vaan nakab ka
Masti se har nigah tere rukh par bikhar gayi

Mara zamane ne 'Asadullah Khan' tumhe
Wo valvale kahan wo jawani kidhar gayi

—Mirza Ghalib

Song 22

Ai behkabri dil ko diwana bana dena
Har sans ki hasti se begana bana dena
Toota hua dil shama-e-butkhana bana dena
Purshor ghataon ko mamnoon na hone do
Tumko bhi to aata hai diwana bana dena
Tamheed-e kharabi ki taqmil kharabi hai
Ek but ka banana hai butkhana bana dena
Khud kisa-e-gam apna vo tah kiya maine
Duniya nai bahut chaha afsana bana dena
'Seemab' yehi jane garmiy-e-mohabat hai
Insan ko hum anjam-e-parwana banµa dena

—Seemab

II

Other All-Time Favourites

(Alaap)
Jhulana jhulavo ree, jhulana jhula, jhulavo ree,
Ambuva kee daree pe koyal bole ama,
Haan, haan, haan, re koyal bole.
Kook kook jiya re, jhulana jhulavo ree,
Jhulana jhulavo ree, jhulana jhulav.

Nanheen nanheen boond, boondaniyan—
Nanheen nanheen boondaniyan,
Nanheen Nanheen boond, boondaniyan—
Barkha phuhaar, ab-hoon na aaye balamva,
Jhulana jhulavo ree—jhulana jhula.
Jhulana jhulavo ree—
Jhulana jhulav, jhulana jhulav, jhulana jhulav

(This is one of the earliest songs, by K.L. Saigal, recorded in February 1933.)

* * *

Baalam aaye baso more man mein—baalam
Saawan aaya tum na aaye—
Tum bin rasiya kachhu naa bhaaye—
Man mein morey hook uthat jab,
    koyal kookat ban mein
Baalam aaye baso more man mein—
Sooratiya jaakee matwaaree,
    Patree kamariya umariya baalee,
Ek naya sansaar basaa hai,
    jinke do nainan mein,
Baalam aaye baso more man mein,

* * *

Dukh ke
Dukh ke ab din beetat naaheen,
Sukh ke din they ek swapan thaa—
Ab din beetat naaheen,
    Morey ab din beetat naaheen,
Dukh ke ab din beetat naaheen, hoon, hoon, hoon . . .
Naa main kisee kaa, naa koi meraa,
Chhaya chaaron or andhera,
Ab kachhu soojhat naaheen,
Morey ab din beetat naaheen,
Dukh ke, dukh ke, dukh ke

* * *

Piye jaa, aur piye jaa,
Zindgi ka gham khaaye, teree balaa.

Piya jaa, aur piye jaa.
Botal uthaa, kaag udaa,
Arey, zindagi kaa yahee hai muddaa,
Piye jaa, aur piye jaa.
Jitnee pee sakta hai pee le,
Arey do din aur bhee jag mein jee le,
        hey, hey, hey, hey . . . .
Sochta hai kya, aur piye jaa
Aakbat kee baatein jaane koi kya
Khair jo hoga, dekha jaayega,
Arey, ab to piye jaa.

* * *

Ik bangla bane nyara,
Rahe kunba jisme sara,
Ik bangla bane nyara.
Sone ka bangla, chandan ka jangla,
Vishwakarm ke dwara, vishwakarm ke dwara,
Ati sundar pyara pyara,
Ik bangla bane nyara, ik bangla bane nyara.
Itna ooncha bangla hoye, maano gagan ka taara,
Jispe chadhke indradhanush pe
        jhoola jhoole chand hamara
Bhandar hoye lachhmee ke haathon mein saara,
Paaye ab jee bhar ke sukh jisne vipat uthayee.

* * *

Prem ka hai is jag mein panth nirala,
Prem to hai duniya mein karan dukh ka.
Premee ko hotaa hai anubhav sukh kaa
Sheetal pawan hai usko prem kee jwala—2
Prem kaa hai is jag mein panth niraalaa.
Prem japan kee jag mein reet hai nyaaree,
Ansuan ke mankon par prem pujaaree,
Ro ro kar japtaa hai prem kee maalaa.
Prem kaa hai is jag mein panth niraalaa.
Paagal premee ab too kyyn rotaa hai?
Prem kaa to aisaa hee phal hotaa hai.

Pehle kaahe na toone dekhaa bhaalaa,
   Pehle kaahe na tooe dekhaa bhaalaa,
     Pehle kaahe na toone dekhaa bhaalaa.

Kisne—, ye sab khel rachaayaa? Kisne ye sab saaj sajaayaa?
Apne aap sabhee kuchh karke,
Apnaa aap chhipaayaa—, kisne
Komal Komal pyaare paudhe—, dhaan paan matwaare paudhe
Inke oopar aakar chhidkee rang roop kee maayaa—2
Apne aap sabhee kuchh karke, apnaa aap chhipaayaa,
Apnaa aap chhipaayaa, kisne
Andhere mein sote the ye, bilkul besudh hote the ye—2
Neendpuree ke madmaaton ko neend se aan jagaayaa—2
Apne aap sabhee kuchh karke, apnaa aap chhipaayaa,
Apnaa aap chhipaayaa, kisne
Haraa bharaa gulzaar khilaa hai, sarson kaa sansaar khilaa hai
Dekh dekh mann mein sukh hovat, ankhiyan noor samaayaa—2
Apne aap sabhee kuchh karke, apnaa aap chhipaayaa,
Apnaa aap chhipaayaa, kisne, kisne
Baabul moraa, naihar chhooto hee jaaye—2,
Baabul moraa, moraa naihar chhooto hee jaaye
Baabul moraa naihar chooto jaaye
Baabul moraa naihar chhooto hee jaaye
Chaar kahaar mile moree doliyaa sajaavein re
Chaar kahaar mile moree doliyaa sajaavein
Chaar kahaar mile moree doliyaa sajaavein re
Moraa apnaa begaanaa chhooto jaaye,
Baabul moraa naihar chhooto hee jaaye.
Anganaa to parbat bhayaa aur dehree bhayee bides
Anganaa to parbat bhayaa haa aur dehree bhayee bides
Le baabul ghar aapno, main chalee piyaa ke des,
Baabul moraa naihar chhooto jaaye
Baabul moraa naihar chhooto hee jaaye.

As Ss, haa Ss, haa Ss,
Karoon kyaa aas niraas bhayee—4,
Diyaa bujhe phir se jal jaaye,
   raat andheree jaaye din aaye—2

Mit-tee aas hai jot ankhiyan kee—2
Samjho gayee to gayee
Karoon kyaa aas iraas bhayee—3
Jab naa kisee ne raah sujhaayee,
    dil se ik aawaaz ye aayee—2
Himmat baandh sambhal badh aage, rok naheen
    hai koi—2
Kaho naa aas niraas bhayee, kaho naa aas niraas bhayee.
Karnaa hogaa khoon kaa paanee,
    denaa hogee ar qurbaanee
Himmat hai itnee to samajh le—2
    aas bandhegee nayee—2
Kaho naa aas niraas bhayee,
    Kaho naa aas niraas bhayee
      Kaho naa aas niraas bhayee

Main kyaa jaanoon kyaa jaadoo hai, jaadoo hai, jaadoo hai
Main kyaa jaanoon kyaa jaadoo hai,
In do matwaale nainon mein.
    jaadoo hai, jaadoo hai, jaadoo hai
Main kyaa jaanoon kyaa jaadoo hai
Ik ek athaah saagar-saa hai—2,
In do matwaale nainon mein,
    jaadoo hai, jaadoo hai, jaadoo hai
Main kyaa jaanoon kyaa jaadoo hai
Mann poochh rahaa hai ab mujhse,
    nainon ne kahaa hai kyaa tujhse—2
Jab nain mile nainon ne kahaa, nainon ne kahaa,
Jab nain mile nainon ne kahaa,
Ab nain basenge nainon mein,
Main kaa jaanoon kyaa jaadoo hai, jaadoo hai, jaadoo hai
In do matwaale nainon mein.
    jaadoo hai, jaadoo hai, jaadoo hai
Main kyaa jaanoon kyaa jaadoo hai

So jaa, so jaa,
So jaa raajkumaaree so jaa—2
So jaa main balihaaree so ja,

So jaa raajkumaaree so jaa
So jaa meethe sapne aayein,
    sapnon mein pee daras dikhaayein—2
Udne waalaa ghodaa laayen, ghode par tumko bithlaayen
Udkar roop nagar mein jaayein—2
Roopnagar kee sakhiyaan aayein—2,
Sakhiyaan aayein khoob sajaayein, raajaa jee maalaa pehnaayein
Raajaa jee maalaa pehnaayein,
Choomein maang tihaaree, so jaa,
So jaa raajkumaree so jaa,
So jaa raajkumaree so jaa.

Hey, deewaanaa hoon, deewaanaa hoon,
Raahat se main begaanaa hoon—2
Deewaanaa hoon, deewaanaa hoon,
Raahat se main begaanaa hoon—2.
Dil ko kaise behalaaun main.
Haan, ye zakhm kise dikhlaaun main
Ye zakhm kise dikhlaaun main
Aanzoo sun sun kar hanste hain
Kyaa dardbharaa of saanaa hoon—2
Aayee na bahaar khizaan hee sahee—2
Ujde dil mein armaan hee sahee—2
Hairaan hoon ke aakhir kyaa hoon main—2
Aabaad hoon yaa veeraanaa hoon—2
Ghaayal hoon tumse door hoon main—2
Par phoonk chukaa majboor hoon main—2
Ai shamaa balaayen le aakar—2
Aakhir main bhee parwaanaa hoon—3

Din soonaa sooraj binaa aur chandaa bin rain
Ghar soonaa deepak inaa, jyoti bina do nain
Diyaa jalaao jagmag jagmag—2
Diyaa jalaao, diyaa jalaao, diyaa jalaao
Diyaa jalaao, diyaa jalaao, jagmag jagmag
Diyaa jalaao jagmag jagmag, diyaa jalaao

Saras suhaagan sun ree, saras suhaagan sun ree—2
Tere mandir mein dekh andheraa—2
Rooth na jaaye piyaa teraa, rooth na
  jaaye piyaa teraa, aa Ssssssssssss
Diyaa jalaao, diyaa jalaao, diyaa jalaao, diyaa jalaao,
Piyaa manaao, diyaa jalaao, piyaa manaavo, manaavo, jalaao
Jagmag jagmag jagmag jagmag jagmag jagmag
  Diyaa jalaao

Do nainaan mataare tihaare, ham par zulam karein,
  hm par zulam karein—2
Nainon mein rahein to sudh budh khoyein—2
Chhipein to, chhipein to chain harein,
Do nainaan, do nainaan, matwaare tihaare,
Ham par zulam karein, ham par zulam karein
Tan tan ke chalaayein teer, nas-2 mein, nas-2 mein uthaayein peer,
Tan tan ke chalaayein teer, nas nas mein uthaayein peer,
Madbhare raseele nithur bade, naa darein na dheer dharein,
Do nainaan matwaare tihaare,
Ham par zulam karein, ham par zulam karein
Jab hotee ho, jab hotee ho tum us paar,
Mann kee, mann kee beenaa ke baj uth-te hain zor zor se taar—2
Paas aayeen, paas aayeen to aise phool gaye,
Pal chhin mein, pal chhin mein sab kuchh bhool gaye,
Paas aayeen to aise phool gaye,
Pal chhin mein sab kuchh bhoo gaye
Khushiyon ke sote ubal pade, har ang mein rang bhare
Do nainaan matwaare tihaare, ham par zulam karein,
Ham par zulam karein

Ai kaatibe-taqdeer mujhe itnaa bataa de,
Ai kaatibe-taqdeer mujhe itnaa bataa de, itnaa bataa de,
Kyon mujhse khafaa hai too kyaa maine kiyaa hai.
Auron ko khushee mujhko phakat dard-o-ranj-o-gham,
Duniyaa ko hansee aur mujhe ronaa diyaa hai.
Kyaa maine kiyaa hai, kyaa maine kiyaa hai?

Kyun mujhse khafaa hai too kyaa maine kiyaa hai
Hisse mein sabke aayeen hain,
    Hisse mein sabke aayeen hain rangeen bahaarein
Badbakhtiyaan lekin mujhe sheeshe mein utaarein,
Peete hain, peete hain log rozo-shab
    musarraton kee maya
Main hoon ke sadaa khoone-jigar maine piyaa hai,
Kyaa maine kiyaa hai, kyaa maine kiyaa hai?
Thaa jinke dam qadam se ye aabaad aashiyaan
Wo chehchahaatee, wo chehchahaatee bulbulein
    jaane gayeen kahaan,
Jugnoo kee chamak hai na sitaaron kee roshanee,
Is ghupp and here mein hai meree jaan par banee,
Kyaa thee, kyaa thee, kyaa thee khataa
    ke jiskee sazaa toone mujhko dee,
Kyaa thaa, kyaa thaa gunaah ke jiskaa badlaa
mujhse liyaa hai
Kyaa maine kiyaa hai, kyaa maine kiyaa hai?
Kyun mujhse khafaa hai too, kyaa maine kiyaa hai

Jab dil hee toot gayaa, jab dil hee toot gayaa,
Ham jee ke kyaa karenge, ham jee ke kyaa karenge
Jab dil hee toot gayaa, jab dil hee toot gayaa.
Ulfat kaa diyaa hamne is il mein jalaayaa thaa—2
Ummeed ke phoolon se is ghar ko sajaayaa thaa—2
Ik bhedee loot gayaa, ik bhedee loot gayaa
Ham jee ke kyaa karenge, ha jee ke kyaa karenge
Jab dil hee toot gayaa.
Maaloom naa thaa itnee mushqil hain
    mere raahein mushqil hain meree raahein—2
Armaan ke bahe aansoo, hasrat ne bharee aahein—2
Har saathee chhoot gayaa, har saathee chhoot gayaa,
Ham jee ke kyaa karenge, ham jee ke kyaa karenge
Jab dil hee toot gayaa.

Toot gaye sab sapne mere, toot gaye,
Toot gaye sab sapne mere,

Ye do nainaan saawan bhaadon, barsein saanjh savere
Toot gaye sab sapne mere.
Dard ne jee par thes lagaayee, tootaa jo dil aawaaz ye aayee—2
Sukh ki tamanna karne waale, sukh nahin bhaag mein tere,
Toot gaye sab sapne mere, ye do nainaan saawan bhaadon,
      barsein saanjh savere, toot gaye sab sapne mere.
Dukh ke sataaye, sukh ke deewaane, dekh rahe the
      khaab suhaane—2
Aankh khulee to aas ke badle yaas khadee thee ghere,
Toot gaye sab sapne mere, ye do nainaan saawan bhaadon,
      barsein saanjh savere, toot gaye sab sapne mere.

As Ss,
Shamaa kaa jalnaa hai yaa sozashe parwaanaa hai—2,
Chand lafzon mein yahee ishq kaa afsaanaa hai—2,
Shamaa kaa jalnaa hai.
Ye junoon hai ki yahaan tak meraa badh jaaye junoon,
Ye junoon hai ki meraa yahaan tak badh jaaye junoon,
Hans ke deewaangee keh de ke ye deewaanaa hai—2,
Shamaa kaa jalnaa hai.
Dil shikastaa liye baithaa hai umangon kaa hujoom—2,
Ek toote huye paimaane mein maikhaanaa hai—2,
Shamaa kaa jalnaa hai.
Aabalaa dil kaa tasallee ke liye hai 'Hasrat'—2,
Yahee saaghar, yahee sheeshaa, yahee paimaanaa hai—2.

As, Ss,
Hari bin koi kaam na aayo,
Is jhoothee maayaa ke kaaran heeraa janam ganvaayo,
Hari bin koi kaam na aayo.
Stree kahe main sang chaloongee,
      khons khons dhan khaayo—2,
Chaltee ber mod mukh baithee palak na ek lagaayo.
Hari bin koi kaam na aayo.
Sab snehee sneh karat hain, in hee ke haath bikaayo,
Toot gayaa jab kanth se doraa, ral mil phoonk jalaayo.
Hari bin kou kaam na aayo.

Maayaa sagee na mann sagaa
   aur sagaa na ye sansaar—2,
'Laal Daas' is jeev kaa sagaa wo surjanhaar,
Hari bin kou kaam na aayo.

Soon after getting this bhajan recorded, Saigal Saheb brought the recording home with him and this bhajan could not be issued on any gramophone disc. The full text of the bhajan has been presented here after listening to the rare recording.

Appendix D
Synopses of Some
Famous Films
(As published in booklets)

Puran Bhakt
A New Theatres'
Super Production

The Story

In the hoary days of India's glorious past, centuries and centuries ago, a powerful King of the name of Silwan ruled over Sialkote and its neighbouring districts. Of King Silwan, it was said: for many years he nursed a grief which was shared by his royal spouse Maharani Ichhra and that grief was the grief of childless parents longing for the advent of one who would be able to carry on the name of his father's house. After years of prayer and acts of penance and religious offerings to the deities, it seemed that the happiness of parenthood was at last to be theirs, for Maharani Ichhra bore King Silwan a male child and great was the rejoicing throughout the Kingdom. On the day the child is born, the cup of happiness is dashed from the lips of the fond parents by the Raj Guru who informs the King that it is ordained in the books of destiny that they must not cast their eyes on their son until he had achieved sixteen summers, under pain of losing him for ever.

Thus it is that the young prince, who has been named Puran, is brought up under the care and the training of the Raj Guru and sees nothing of his parents whatsoever. The birth of a prince and heir to King Silwan has been the cause of much disappointment to Mahipat, Silwan's Senapati, who had hoped to succeed him had he died without issue. And during these sixteen years, Mahipat broods and plots to bring about the destruction of Puran, and, with this end in view, he has spread from time to time rumours of the wild escapades in which Puran has been wont to indulge and these have reached the ears of the King who, in the course of these years, has taken unto himself a second Queen, much younger than he, named Luna.

The longed-for-day arrives and Puran goes forth at last to Sialkote to meet his parents. When the handsome young prince appears in his father's court, the young Queen Luna, tired of an old man's love, finds her heart aflame for her step-son, and endeavours, by all wiles known to woman, to kindle in Puran's heart a reciprocal affection. Amazed, ashamed and horrorstruck, simple Puran repulses her overtures and leaves behind him that which is more deadly than the most dangerous snake in the world — a woman who hates!

Luna does not take long to have her revenge and going up to her doting husband, she indignantly denounces Puran for molesting her. Now, Silwan having heard of his escapades from Mahipat gets enraged at this latest piece of vandalism on Puran's part, flies into a rage and orders Mahipat to fling Puran into a well after cutting off both his hands. Only too gladly does Mahipat carry out his Sire's order. But Puran is rescued by a mystic ascetic Guru Gorakshnath who joins together again his severed hands and takes Puran away to bring him up as his disciple.

In order to see how far his disciple was able to carry out his vow of renunciation of the world, Gorakshnath sends Puran on an errand to the court of the beautiful Rani Sundara, who rules over an Amazon kingdom and who falls so much in love with Puran at the very first sight that she tries even to invoke the help of Gorakshnath himself in order to win him. In the meantime, Mahipat, feeling that the time was ripe, rebels against King Silwan and dethrones and imprisons him. Then Silwan's followers appeal to the Amazons to go to their assistance in restoring him to the throne. Gorakshnath, also learning of Silwan's predicament, sends Puran post-haste to aid his father, and with the help of his Guru and Rani Sundara, Puran succeeds in overpowering Mahipat and restoring his father to the throne. He sees his mother once again, blind through sorrow at losing him, and invokes Gorakshnath's aid to restore her eyesight. After which, he marries Rani Sundara, being touched by her love for him but the vow he has taken cannot be broken and so Bhakt Puran renounces his claim to the throne, installing his half-brother in his place, and, leaving his wife and his parents, he takes the long unending road of *ahimsa* and renunciation.

Yahoodi ki Ladki
As Filmed by the New Theatres Ltd, Calcutta

The Jew! Accursed, homeless, wandering scion of the house of Moses, from time immemorial, since the day when Moses in impotent rage and anger cursed him for his faithlessness . . . he has been the target of civilized mankind's unreasonable hatred and contempt. Wave upon wave of persecution has swept over him, generation after generation, but still the Jew has not expiated his ancient crime, still he wanders with his hand against every man and every man's hand against him.

Even as it is today so it was in the days of the great, powerful and arrogant Roman Emperors. Even in those days, the Jew was marked out for special humiliation for no other reason but that he was a Jew.

But while he has been thus accursed, the Jew has been blessed with patience, forbearance, thrift and intelligence. His culture and his religion have always been supreme to him; and in his heart of hearts he has smiled contemptuously at his persecution and has bided his time to humiliate their arrogance and bring them to the dust at his knees.

And Ezra, the Jewish merchant prince, living in the days of ancient Rome, is not an exception to his endless race. Incessantly persecuted by the arrogant hatred of Brutus, the Roman High Priest, harassed and robbed at every turn by contemptuous Romans simply because he is a Jew, Ezra nevertheless manages to hold his own by the power of his wealth, until the day when his only son, the apple of his eye and his consolation in life, Yameen, happens, while playing with a catapult to hit by accident, the dreaded Brutus as he passes by house of Ezra.

It is enough! This is the excuse that Brutus had been seeking to crush the Jew and to break his heart completely. A Jewish boy, be he only seven years of age, had actually had the termerity 'to attack' and to hit the High Priest of Rome! What greater excuse could there be for the infliction of the greatest punishment imaginable on this lad? Torn away from his home by brutal soldiers this tender, trembling and innocent boy is thrown to the lions and torn to pieces by the beasts to the accompanying plaudits of the cruel, unthinking Roman crowd.

2

'An eye for an eye, a tooth for a tooth!' According to this relentless creed of the Jews, Elias, Ezra's devoted slave, vows to avenge this ruthless killing of innocent Yameen, this murder of a loving father's only child, and at night, he manages to break into Brutus' house and, kidnapping his only child Decia, he brings her to Ezra so that Ezra may take revenge. But Ezra, pining for his beloved child, sees in Decia consolation and taking her to his heart he brings her up as his own daughter.

Fifteen years roll by and Hanna, the daughter of the Jew, grown into beautiful womanhood, is molested by Roman soldiers one day, when Marcus the Roman prince happens to be passing by in disguise. Marcus rescues Hanna and brings her to her home, and from that day there is born a deep love between them, which causes this Roman prince, engaged to be married to his royal cousin Princess Octavia, to forget everything in his mad infatuation for this daughter of a Jew. Dressed as a Jew, he is made welcome at Hanna's house, until one day Hanna's suspicions are aroused by certain incidents, and she tackles Marcus as to his identity. Cornered, Marcus admits that he is a Roman, but pleads in defence his love for Hanna and eventually succeeds in persuading Hanna to agree to elope with him.

Just as they are on the point of eloping, however, Ezra, who has heard all that has passed between the two, faces them in righteous anger, but agrees eventually to allow Marcus to wed Hanna on condition that Marcus gives up his religion to prove his love for Hanna. Marcus refuses and Ezra turns him out of the house, and in anger curses him.

Marcus decides to bow down to fate and marry Princess Octavia. Celebrations proceed apace until the day of the actual marriage when Ezra, taking presents for the happy couple, takes Hanna along with him to witness this great occasion. Hanna recognizes Marcus as her one-time lover, and, regardless of consequences, accuses Marcus before the Emperor of having been faithless to her and appeals to him for justice. In spite of Brutus' interpretations that the law could not apply to princes of the royal blood, the King orders Marcus to be arrested and to stand his trial. Before the day of the trial arrives, the proud Octavia, begging on bended knees to the daughter of the Jew, succeeds in getting her to agree to retract her statement and thus saves Marcus from punishment and unhappiness. True to her promise Hanna retracts her statement, Marcus is set free, and Brutus, in triumphant hatred, orders both Ezra and Hanna to be burnt at the stake for perjury against the prince.

This is the day for which the patient Jew has waited all his life. This is to be the day of his supreme triumph when he would see his relentless enemy humbled to the dust even though he himself were on the point of death.

At the execution ground, where Brutus has gone to enjoy the sight of the destruction of the hated Jew and his daughter. Ezra recalls to Brutus' mind the kidnapping of his only child Decia and states that he, and he alone, knows the whereabouts of this girl who is still alive.

Distracted with love for his long-lost child, Brutus begs, cajoles, threatens, and again begs Ezra in humility to disclose the girl's whereabouts. Ezra agrees on condition that immediately after his doing so Brutus would command that first Hanna, and then Ezra, would be burnt on the spot. Brutus thoughtlessly agrees and it is then that the Jew discloses Hanna's true identity.

Upon his knees, humbled to the dust, the proud Roman falters and begs Ezra to allow him to retract his promise. But neither his pleadings, nor those of the king, Marcus and Octavia can move either the old Jew or Hanna, who both insist on the punishment being carried out. In the midst of this dramatic impasse there occurs a sudden diversion. Suddenly and without warning, lo! There is heard a wonderful voice and down the steps of the dungeon there comes a saintly figure who speaks to Hanna of a beautiful world of spiritual existence and exhorts her to renounce this materialistic world. And Hanna, uplifted and exulting in this message, leaves the dungeon and all assembled, for renunciation and the land of Ultima Thule for which mankind is ever striving but which is never reached.

Chandidas

Gopinath was the zamindar of a village. He was rich and mighty. He was the patron of the village Brahmins who considered him to be their champion of religion and justice. But underneath his highly polished manners and religious-mindedness, the zzmindar was a debauch of the lowest type and a tyrant of the highest order! He was a devil incarnate. With the help of Sarju, his able and cunning lieutenent, the zamindar could prepare the blackest crime with impunity — and then smile complacently!

Baiju, the washerman of the village, lived happily with his simple wife Kusum and his sister Rami. Rami was young and beautiful and her charms were irresistible

There was the temple of Basuli in the village. Chandidas, the disciple of Acharya, was the priest of the temple, Chandidas was imaginative, a lover of humanity, and above all he was a lover of truth.

Day after day, in the compound of the temple, Rami was to be seen sweeping the temple yard and day after day, within the temple Chandidas was found to be going on with his priestly duties. Between Rami and Chandidas were the hard stone-steps of the temple. Between them there were also the barriers of caste and society, which were harder to climb than the stone steps of the temple.

As is usual, Rami's irresistible charms cast a spell on the lustful eyes of Gopinath, and Gopinath, with the help of the right-hand man in all his nefarious activities, Sarju, was determined to get Rami at any cost. All networks of temptations to win over Rami were in vain and Gopinath in despair had to take recourse to force, and kidnapped Rami to his place. While he was about to outrage Rami in a private room, Kalyani, the zamindar's wife and a living ideal of Hindu womanhood, stepped in and rescued Rami from Gopinath's clutches.

2

The zamindar — baffled and infuriated — started a series of persecutions on Rami and her brother's family, which climaxed in the burning of poor Baiju's hut. When the hut was burning, Rami compelled Chandidas to throw off all barriers of caste and creed. He even risked his life for his great love.

Gopinath was not idle and through his manipulations Chandidas was considered to be impure and fallen from the path of religion and society. Ultimately he was forced to concede to the proposals of a penance 'prayaschitya' for . . . for what else, but his connection with the washerwoman?

Rami heard of Chandidas on the point of doing the penance but she could not believe it — it was impossible for her to do it! Anyway she wanted to get the truth direct from Chandidas. She ran to the scene of penance and reached the scene after suffering many a physical torture in her way—Gopinath took all possible care to prevent Rami from seeing Chandidas before the penance was done and posted men at every corner. But love is all-powerful—and Rami stood face to face with Chandidas.

The Brahmins shuddered, Gopinath stood baffled and roared within himself. Chandidas stood up, leaving the penance unfinished, took Rami in his embrace and then went out of the temple, out of the village—out of the rigid and unkind conventions of society.

Everything—society, caste and convention—lay behind. The two moved out to the realm of love.

Caste and convention frowned—but truth—who will say if it frowned or smiled?

Devdas

Devdas is a story of hearts.

Devdas was a young man—born and brought up amidst the quietitude of a village—rich but unostentatious. He was the son of a rich zamindar but fate made him love Parbati, the daughter of a poor neighbour.

Love knows no reason. So Devdas loved Parbati and Parbati loved Devdas—in spite of social barriers.

Little did they know how unsurmountable they were and little did they guess what the future had in store for them.

A time came when Devdas had to part from his childhood playmate Parbati and go to the city for his education and his polish. And the parting?—It was cruel. Devdas wanted to revolt but Father, Mother, duty, society demanded that he should go to Calcutta to complete his education and get enlightened . . . Separation? Love? Silly sentiments! . . . Devdas had to go . . .

And Parbati? She shed many a bitter tear—and prepared herself for her marriage, as arranged by her parents and by society. The bridegroom was a big zamindar of a neighbouring district. The Rai Sahib was old, and was marrrying for the second time, and was the father of big sons and daughters—and society did not understand why Parbati should not be happy.

Devdas heard about it, just as Parbati had . . . One final effort against overwhelming odds . . .

Society won and broke two hearts in the battle . . . Devdas returned to Calcutta broken-hearted while Parbati went with her old husband—her life blasted with one stroke of fortune—to suffer silently and drag along her miserable existence without the faintest ray of hope . . .

Devdas went back to Calcutta. He was rich. He was unhappy. Easy friends with easier virtues gathered round him. Chunilal, an adventurer, showed him the way. Wine came and with it came—women.

And, Devdas met Chandra, a girl who sold her body to earn an existence. Chandra found Devdas different—different from her usual customs. Because, Devdas drank to drown his sorrows and because Devdas hated her. In Devdas she found something common—they both hated her profession . . . Chandra fell in love with Devdas . . . And, Devdas—well, how could Devdas love a women like Chandra? . . . Another broken heart who saved her soul and purified it in love . . .

Devdas drank wine hoping to drown his soul in it . . .

Time passed—days—months—years . . .

Parbati heard about Devdas and came to him. Parbati wanted Devdas to promise that he would give up drinking. Devdas asked—'Why?' and this 'why' had no answer . . . Devdas promised that he would come to Parbati for her help, for her pity, for her tears—at last, once before his death.

Devdas invited death and death accepted the invitation readily . . . Diseased and drunken Devdas walked the pavements while far, far away Parbati shed silent tears in the recluse of her new home. Parbati lived. Parbati worked. Parbati was dutiful. Parbati was the ideal wife. People worshipped her. Her husband adored her. But they did not know that her soul was dead. She existed but she did not live . . .

Morning came and went in the peaceful village of Parbati and once the peace was disturbed by the finding of the dead body of a man. The small village was stirred up by the event and police enquired and found the man to be Devdas. He had travelled all night, they said, and had broken down. A few pieces of wood—a flame—and Devdas was no more . . .

And, Parbati? She heard from behind the high surrounding walls of her home—she heard that her Devdas was dead.

President

'Hush! Hush! To your work, boys! The tiger!!'

Thus she, Prabhavati, the President of 'The Prabhavati Cotton Mills

Ltd', was feared by many and respected by all in the mill. But she was a mere child of sixteen when her father left her a small and modest establishment. Since then, twelve summers found her working hard and making it into a gigantic organization. But all the springs passed by unnoticed, the existence of any world other than that of work . . . workers and machines she knew not. What is more, she became a machine herself without realizing it. Good workers were rewarded with the same coolness with which she dismissed others. So, when Prakash, an ordinary workman took it into his head to make some new designs of 'saris' without being asked to do so, he was taken to task very severely. What an audacity! He dared tell the President that his 'design' was a good one and the machine he was working with was bad and dangerous, and all these on her face! . . . . Naturally Prakash was dismissed. But the same day his warning came true. The man who was given Prakash's job met with an accident which set the President thinking: 'That man was not entirely wrong after all.' Was she sorry then?

Poor Prakash had to support a widowed sister and his young nephew with what he earned from the mill—and that was gone! Worried and exhausted, in search of a new job, he sat under the boundary wall of a house for rest. Who knew that it was a girl's hostel? And a street urchin was playing on the flute. Who knew that it was the Flute of Fate? Thus they met, Prakash and Sheela, as Fate ordained, like the Prince and Princess in a fairytale. When the time came, they parted with the pleasant memories of their meeting in their young hearts.

But the authorities of the college found Sheela guilty of the most infamous charges in the history of the college. To retain the dignity of the institution the authorities, therefore, expelled Sheela from the college without offering her any chance whatsoever to explain the situation for which she was the least responsible. Was justice done to her? And who would believe that Sheela was the younger sister of the President of 'The Prabhavati Cotton Mills Ltd'? Much younger, light-hearted, gay and a total contrast to her elder sister in everything except the love they had for each other, each in her own way.

The particular 'design' for which Prakash was dismissed, to everybody's surprise, made the most tremendous hit in the market. The President for the first time in her life was thinking about a dismissed man. 'Was justice done to him?' And that was also the opinion of Dr Sethi, a physician and an erudite scholar who was more a friend than simply a Director of the mill; something more than a friend, a perfect gentleman who had been very patiently waiting for years with a secret and tender feeling for the President in his heart. Out of employment, Prakash was having a very hard time in trying to hide this fact from his sister. But Dinu, a fellow worker of Prakash and a true comrade, urged him to go to the President and beg for his job back. 'Vanity and pride with an empty stomach! What nonsense!' was the sound logic of Dinu. But Prakash was saved from the trouble.

The President herself came one day. And before the two friends could get over their confusion owing to this, came the incredible news of Prakash's re-instalment as the head of the 'design' department! Amazed and bewildered, the two friends looked at each other!

No more poverty, no more worries. Prakash, while returning home with loads of presents for his sister, nephew and Dinu, was almost run over by a car. Whom did he see in the car . . . ?

'The Princess!'

And Sheela saw 'The Prince!'

The next time when Fate played her usual trick on them, they were pleasantly surprised to meet each other at the President's office. The elder sister herself introduced the younger to Prakash knowing nothing about the love that was growing between them secretly.

The bigger the mill became, higher rose Prakash. Position and honour were bestowed on him, till one day, he was made the General Manager of the mill from where he was once dismissed. Unexpected though unlikely it might appear, the President was found liking the man not only for his efficient hardwork, nor was it due to pity or kindness but for something else; some other interest was behind it all. Was it spring this time? Did this man remind her of spring?

Dinu was then not altogether wrong, may be a little exaggerated, to make merry over his dream that some day in the very near future, the entire mill will be theirs; he meant Prakash's, if things went on like this.

Good time . . . abundance! Prakash's sister thought that it was time that Prakash got married. 'Wait,' said Dinu, 'Not only a wife for Prakash will I give you, but a kingdom along with it!'

'Sheela should get married also,' thought her elder sister. But whom should she marry? Young and rich Bikram Sethi, a cousin of Dr Sethi had just returned home from abroad. Did Sheela and Bikram seem to be friendly with each other? Bikram, of course, like many other young men returning home after a stay abroad, found everything wrong and ugly in his country, but found nothing wrong or ugly about Miss Roy.

On the contrary, he found her very agreeable. But how could anybody know that Sheela was dreaming all the time about the Prince Charming of the fairytale! How little we understand each other!

Sheela thought that 'Didi' had changed. Didi of all persons tried to look beautiful! Why—of course she had the same right to be in love and happy as anyone else. Was Dr Sethi then going to be the lucky man at last and be rewarded for his patience, waiting and perseverance?

When the birthday aniversary arrived, Dr Sethi, along with other friends, arranged to celebrate it in a novel way. A drama was composed by no less a person than Dr Sethi himself, and was being staged in the drawing room of the President. Everything looked bright and gay, but, behind the screen, progressed more rapidly the drama of their real life than the drama on the stage. Incidents there happened quick and unexpected. The elder and the younger sisters found themselves to be the rivals for the love of the same man. The drama on the stage of course stopped, but the real drama of life took such a severe turn that no human hand could control it!

That midnight found Sheela leaving her 'Didi.' Didi failed to understand her. And that midnight found Prakash misunderstand the strange misbehaviour of Sheela. But why? Sheela was no doubt a child, but the same spirit lived in her as in 'Didi.' Sheela was making the sacrifice. She wanted her 'Didi' to be happy. But Sheela did not know that 'Didi' could never think of her own happiness when Sheela's was at stake. Nothing existed in the whole world that could ever be in the path of the stream of love that was flowing in them, nor anything that had the power enough to separate them even for a moment. Such was the love between the two sisters.

Worried and upset, 'Didi' could no longer be herself in spite of all her efforts. No wonder that it vitally affected her physically as well as mentally.

Baffled and broken-hearted Prakash took recourse to his work like a drowning man catching at a straw. He worked day and night himself and made others work. He had no right to make others suffer for his own suffering. But love sometimes makes one blind. Dinu reasoned and argued but to no avail. Prakash had no sight to see and no mind to think, Dinu was as dear a friend as fierce a foe. So he stood against his dear Prakash for the safety of the mill—for the welfare of his comrades. Workers revolted. All against one. Prakash was in danger.

Disorder everywhere. The situation grew more and more perilous and disastrous; even more, it became a matter of life and death, particularly for Prakash.

What did the President do when she heard of this? Where was Sheela and what did she do? Could Dr Sethi help them in any way? What could other people do in such a case?

Dharti Mata

Industrialization of our country may confer some social benefit, but I maintain that agriculture, widespread agriculture, agriculture with improved methods and implements, and farming, is our country's primary need and the salvation of the starving and half-fed millions in the villages; I feel my duty is amongst them. 'Brother Ajay, you may go to England and prosecute your studies in mining. Let me remain here.' The rich Ajay tries to dissuade his poor but best friend Asoke from this resolve and entreats him to come along to England to study together. Asoke remains adamant and steadfast. In the face of a national scourge and in an effort to wipe it out, Asoke is not shaken and the entreaties and requests of a life-long friend and his beautiful sister, Pratibha, fall on deaf ears.

Ajay sails for England alone.

Asoke goes to the villages. He inspires a band of spirited young men to accompany him. Chandan, a cousin of Ajay, is sent by Pratibha to help Asoke. Pratibha serenely but secretly loves Asoke. Patriotic Asoke is blind to it.

Big-scale farming is Asoke's ambition. He speaks of this scheme to the villagers. He appeals to them in the name of national and collective prosperity. The villagers are moved and are about to fall in with Asoke, but Chowdhury, the village headman, disapproves of Asoke and his scheme. A typical village despot—always a hindrance rather than an aid to any good cause—finds Asoke and his band an obstacle to his selfish despotic ways and dissuades the villagers from joining Asoke. The poor villagers, heavily in debt to Chowdhury, submissively obey him.

Kunja, a social outcast—for his faulty lay in his inability to give away his daughter Gauri in marriage—joins Asoke. Kunja has a social conscience and his outlook on life is not strictly material. Amongst other reasons he finds some new ethical possibilities in Asoke's adventure.

For lack of practical experience and want of funds they cannot plough or employ skilled labour. Pratibha nobly comes forward to help Asoke in his distress, but Asoke politely refuses his rich friend's sister's offer. Pratibha cannot see her beloved in trouble, a thought strikes her; she employs Chandan to carry the money to Asoke, and extracts a promise from Chandan never to disclose the fact.

In the village, everything seems to be taking a turn for the good. Gauri has enraptured the heart of Asoke, who has fallen head over heels in love with her. The fields show prospects of a bumper crop. But hush! Touch wood. The evil ear has heard. The evil eye has seen. Chowdhury in his invocation to the green-eyed god swears vengeance on Asoke and his crops, and in the dead of night, stealthily marches to the field, bent upon mischief. There is no one to stop him, but his hand of revenge is stopped. He is ashamed of himself. He leaves the village. Chandan, by now a full-fledged member of Asoke's enthusiastic band, brings home the news of Chowdhury's quiet departure and jokingly remarks that Chowdhury has gone on penance.

Pratibha, in all eagerness to see Asoke, speeds to the village. Pratibha meets Gauri. Pratibha returns home happy and Asoke is drawn closer to Gauri.

Both the girls love the same man.

Harvest time. Asoke and his friends have grown a fine, rich crop. But incidentally, the rest of the village has a very bad season. The villagers, who have followed Chowdhury's advice, look upon it as a divine punishment upon themselves. They agree to work with Asoke. Chowdhury comes back to the village. The villagers apprehend danger. But contrary to their fear and apprehension, Chowdhury joins Asoke. Chowdhury goes a step further. He frees the villagers of all debts. He burns their handnotes.

With this powerful combine, the next season Asoke ventures upon farming on a big scale. Chandan brings money. It helps Asoke to replace primitive implements with modern machinery. More fields to plough, more crops to reap. No more jealousies. No more quarrels. One big co-operative effort. One for all and all for one.

In the midst of this all, Ajay returns from England. He is informed of a first-class coal mine. Ajay is eager to work it. He learns that the mine lies directly under Asoke's fields. He hears from Pratibha of the splendid work being done by Asoke. Ajay refrains from running the mine.

Ajay goes to Asoke in the fields. Asoke's grand effort pleases Ajay. Ajay proposes to purchase the land lest Asoke be dispossessed ever. Ajay's gesture moves Asoke. In his joy, Asoke tells Ajay of his love for Gauri, Ajay is dumbfounded. Dark divisions of Pratibha's collapse come up before his misty eyes. But Pratibha has to be informed, the sooner the better.

Asoke and the little community have staked their all in the huge enterprise. Big fields have been ploughed and tilled. The monsoons are eagerly awaited for. Days pass, weeks pass and there is no rain. Instead there are signs of a drought. The drought increases. Asoke is at his wit's end. Tubewells can still save the situation. Chandan rushes to Pratibha for more money. Pratibha pleads poverty. For she has given her all to Chandan. It is difficult for Chandan to believe rich Pratibha's statement. Tears in Pratibha's eyes endorse her statement. She requests Chandan to approach her brother, Ajay. Chandan refuses to go to one who has no faith in their scheme. The drought is increasing. Chandan returns emptyhanded. The peasants lose all faith in Asoke. They revolt.

Ajay now decides to work the mine in Asoke's village. Ajay offers tempting prices to the villagers. They sell their farms one by one. The collapses of Asoke's ambitious scheme is inevitable. But what happens? Does it collapse?

Street Singer

Drifting on the sea of life, singing in the *mela*s, dancing in the bazaars was Bhulwa, a young urchin, pleasantly naughty but highly sentimental, earning his few annas a day in meal theatricals. A suburb of Calcutta is agog with excitement with the presence of a touring theatrical in the midst of its semi-village quietude. Bhulwa as usual plays his pranks, arouses the ire of the manager, gets a box on his ears, a punch on his nose and a kick in his hind parts. His self-respect hurt, he runs as fast as his small legs can carry him, clings on the ladder of a speeding fire engine and escapes the fury of his persecutor. The fire-engine rushes to extinguish the flames that engulf an orphanage. Bhulwa is an astonished onlooker. Little orphans are being saved—one of them, a sweet little mute, runs away from her tormentor—here again the manager—and literally bumps into Bhulwa. Bhulwa, ever sympathetic with ones smaller than himself, pities the girl and together they run away from the scene of confusion and turmoil. Safe in the peacefulness of a nearby grove, Bhulwa tries to impress upon his ward his greatness and confides in her his ambitions of appearing on the stage of the big theatres of Calcutta. He speaks enthusiastically of the footlights and the limelight. He assures her that he will teach her to sing and dance and together they will win fame and fortune. His enthusiasm waxes and his eloquence takes them deeper into the night, when the cold wind rudely reminds him of his poverty and the scantiness of Monju's clothing.

Bravely, Bhulwa doffs his shirt and wraps it round the shivering Monju and spying some boats nearby, takes refuge from the biting north wind and comfortably they go to sleep in one of the boats. Taking advantage of the high tide, the boatmen push off, unaware of the stowaways, and the morning sees them in a distant village.

Bhulwa and Monju, thrown together by circumstances, develop a strong attachment, singing, dancing, begging, growing up together. They grow and Bhulwa's desire to join the theatre grows. They carefully save the alms they collect from village to village. They buy a harmonium and set out for Calcutta to attain Bhulwa's long-cherished desire and ambition, with great hopes. But Dame Fate is peculiar, and her eccentricities still more peculiar. Bhulwa's hopes are shattered. Monju entreats Bhulwa to return to the village. She speaks of the peace of village life. Bhulwa does not agree. His desire is unquenchable.

Singing on the streets for alms, the golden voice of Monju attracts the attention of Amarchand, the actor-manager of the Diamond Theatre. This profligate, as he is, orders a servant to call the street singer in. Amarchand is astonished to see such a beautiful face matching the golden voice, and to think that they are being wasted on the streets. He gives them a five rupee note and promises Monju a job on the stage and holds out a promise to Bhulwa as well.

Brooding over his losses, pondering over the possibilities of a revival of business if a beautiful girl is found, sat Triloke Nath, the proprietor of the Diamond Theatre, worried and perplexed. Amarchand rushes in with the good news. Triloke Nath and Amarchand go to Monju. Monju's job is confirmed. Promises are held out to Bhulwa. Monju gets her theatrical songs tuned by Bhulwa and is trained by him. Events change

fast. Amarchand has fallen in love with Monju. This love has changed
Amarchand. He has got rid of his vices. He tries to serve Monju. Triloke
Nath tries to seduce Monju, Amarchand saves her. Amarchand explains
to Monju that there is dirt and uncleanliness in all walks of life but one
can live cleanly in any walk of life.

The premiere. Monju's debut. Stage fright. Amarchand encourages
Monju. Monju appeals to Bhulwa. Bhulwa comforts her. Amarchand gives
a bouquet to Monju, Monju gives it to Bhulwa. Bhulwa whispers soft
words of encouragement. Monju enters. Her eyes on Bhulwa, she greets
the audience. The audience greets her. Monju's debut is successful. She
is acclaimed. The Diamond Theatre prospers. Though successful, Monju
does not live the city life. Bhulwa, still hoping for a chance for himself,
persuades her to stay on. He infuses her with spirit. The evolution of Monju
begins. Modern furniture, modern dresses, modern taste. Swollen-headed
with fame, Monju is no longer a village girl. Monju rebukes a servant.
Bhulwa is annoyed at her high-brow manner. He reminds her of her own
days of poverty. Monju does not like the reminder. She leaves for the
theatre. Amarchand, in his desire to possess Monju, turns up a new leaf in
life. He places himself and his all at Monju's disposal. Monju is pleased.
She is carried away by Amarchand's attention and munificence. At times
she forgets Bhulwa; Bhulwa feels this inattention. He bears it silently.
Amarchand keeps Bhulwa in hopes for a job.

One day the music director requests Monju to learn the new tune of
a song, Bhulwa's favourite song; Monju refuses to change the tune. The
music director insists. Monju persists. They argue. Monju declines. Monju
returns home. She does not find Bhulwa at home. She hears that Bhulwa
has fever and has gone out. She cooks some light food for the sick.

Amarchand hears of Monju's refusal to work. He hurries to request
her to return. 'It is the opening night of the new play. They will be ruined.'
Amarchand pleads. A voice is heard on the radio. Monju is pleasantly
surprised hearing Bhulwa's voice on the radio. At the same time Monju
feels hurt because Bhulwa never told her about this engagement at the
radio station. Amarchand entreats Monju to come back and sing the song
in the new tune. Monju, declining, says it will pain Bhulwa if she changed
the tune set by him, and then, suddenly, agrees to the new tune, just to
spite Bhulwa. She believes Bhulwa ignored her when he took up the job
at the radio station. To tease Bhulwa further, she orders the servant to ask
Bhulwa, on his return, to go to the theatre; calculating on his annoyance

when he hears the new tune, not counting upon the grave consequences it may lead to. Bhulwa returns home soaked in rain. The fever has increased. The servant gives Monju's message. Bhulwa hurries to the theatre. The servant requests him to rest with his fever. Bhulwa says that Monju will be nervous without him. He must be near her. She will be encouraged. He goes.

The play has started: Monju nervously awaits Bhulwa. She looks for him in the audience. Bhulwa arrives. Monju sees him. She sings. Bhulwa is surprised. It is not the same time. The Devis are insulted. He cannot bear it. He jumps on the stage. There is confusion. The curtain is dropped. Bhulwa is thrashed and turned out of the theatre. Monju is unaware of the treatment accorded to Bhulwa. On the contrary, she is highly strung and feels insulted at Bhulwa's behaviour in the presence of the big crowd. Monju tells Amarchand that she will never return to Bhulwa. Amarchand is inwardly delighted. Amarchand takes Monju to his house. Monju cannot sleep. She weeps and passes a sleepless night.

Bhulwa returns home. He picks up his old harmonium and speaks to it. 'Monju is lost,' he says. 'Let us find her.' With an old costume of Monju and singing her favourite song on the faithful harmonium, Bhulwa sets out.

Monju comes home to tell Bhulwa that she will never see him again. She does not find Bhulwa. She is upset. Complaints and accusations fly to the winds. Remorses set in. Old love finds its place. Monju telephones Amarchand to come quickly. Amarchand misunderstands. He hurries to her, Monju accompanies Amarchand in his car, her eyes searching for Bhulwa. Amarchand is happy. He thinks she is fleeing with him. Amarchand, with a hidden pride, reminds Monju that she is leaving fame and fortune behind. Monju does not pay heed to his words. There is but one thought in her mind, one object in view. Her eyes scanning, her mind fixed, her heart going out to the one and only Bhulwa. Her one request to Amarchand is to go faster. As for in the road, Monju requests Amarchand to go on the road on which Bhulwa and she had travelled to the city. 'He must have gone on this road. Please hurry. Find him. He is angry. I will lose him.' These words bring the truth home to Amarchand. He realizes. A storm has arisen.

The riverside is reached. Bhulwa's boat can be seen in the distance. Monju's favourite song can be fairly heard through the storm. Monju cries and shouts for Bhulwa. The storm increases. The boat is tossed

about. Monju can still hear the faint music. She cries louder and louder.
The storm rages stronger. The boat is dashed against the banks. Thank
God, it is the nearer bank. Monju rushes to her Bhulwa. Amarchand exits.
Bhulwa is senseless. His hands clining to Monju's old costume, his faithful
harmonium near him. Monju raises Bhulwa's unconscious head to her lap,
Bhulwa opens his eyes. He sees. Monju smiles. Monju looks to the road
leading to the villages and peace. Bhulwa smiles.

Zindagi

It was strangely coincidental that Ratan and Shrimati met at a street-corner
at the dead of night, just when both of them were in search of a safe and
secluded place to give them protection from the watchful eyes of the
passing policeman.

Ratan and Shrimati! Two vagabonds! Yes, they were vagabonds—for
none of them could boast of any ostensible means of livelihood. Ratan
was an MA, and yet he was a 'loafer'; and Shrimati a married woman—a
runaway wife of an inhuman husband. They met, and though the vagabond
did not like a runaway woman accosting him for help and support, he
gradually gave way; and gradually a true friendship—a camaraderie of
'vagabonds' grew up between them.

Days rolled on and they remained no more than two good friends to
each other. The world was bright but their steadily dwindling common
purse reminded them now and then that the world was not all sunshine,
but dark clouds may often envelope the horizon. And when the dark clouds
got darker, they came to a temple to make some easy money.

Temple—the haven of the forlorn. The priest was an amiable personality.
Ratan introduced himself as the secretary of a Charitable Trust, and
Shrimati as a 'Sannyasini' founder of the Charitable Trust. The priest was
overwhelmed. Ratan proposed to the priest that the 'Sannyasini' wanted to
sit by the temple and earn some 'Pranamis', i.e., offerings in cash and kind,
for the benefit of the charities. The priest gladly responded and arranged
things to such perfection that the vagabond pair earned an amount of over
a hundred rupees in the course of only twenty-four hours. Shrimati was
after all a woman and her conscience pricked her, but Ratan, with a calm
composure of mind—and may be in a cynic's vein, taught her to 'cheat
those who wanted to be cheated'.

Taxi—shops—the jingle of money in one's own pocket! That was life and that was excitement! And when the flush of excitement was over, they found themselves settled in a well-furnished flat.

'But why all this? Our idea was not to start a home,' queried Ratan. Shrimati admitted, 'Yes, you are right. We have met to part.'

Ratan muttered again, 'But what will happen to all this? I am a gambler all my life; I'll take a couple of coins and try my luck. But you cannot gamble.'

Shrimati could not answer back. She could not—she would not gamble. She was a woman after all, with a rich father still living—no, why should she gamble? So, the next day they parted. Ratan and Shrimati were again on the street.

Ratan could have gone back to the flat but it was so lonely without Shrimati. Ratan's chain of thought got a shaking when he found himself nearly run over by a rickshaw! Out popped from the rickshaw a fellow—Ratan's pal, Dulal, who was neither a cynic nor a very poor man. He believed in the virtues of wine. He could successfully induce his friend to accompany him to the houses of his mistress and after some mad revelry, Dulal and Ratan come back to Ratan's flat to pass the rest of the night. Dulal was fully drunk! However, he got a decisive shock at the sudden appearance of Shrimati and the climax was reached when Shrimati turned Dulal out of the house. Shrimati hated drunkards more than poison.

'He is a friend of mine. Do you know he has no place to go?' Ratan remonstrated.

'No,' said Shrimati, 'but I know this much that a moral-wreck can have no place under my roof.'

Silence prevailed. Ratan understood. Shrimati apologized mutely and so did Ratan. They became friends again.

Then after a while asked Ratan, 'Why you have come back again?' Ratan would not have ventured this question if he only knew that love to a man was a thing apart, but to a woman it was her whole existence.

'A woman's mind has peculiar pranks. I was myself wondering as to why I came back. Do you know that in spite of all the insults and oppressions meted out to me by my husband—at the dead of night, I feel tempted to go and peep through the window to see if my husband is safe and happy. What do you call it? Love? Foolishness? Or what?'

Ratan wondered. She felt tired and Ratan—her friend—sang her to sleep . . . And then they parted again.

Ratan and Dulal were together once more. Dulal did really love Ratan and protested when Ratan wanted to go back to the flat again. Dulal thought it was a crime to live with someone else's wife, even though entirely separated from each other within the premises. Ratan, however, came back to the flat.

Ratan found a chit on the door-step—it was Shrimati's letter. It contained news, all about herself. Shrimati's father had died. She had inherited a fortune. She had devoted her life to philanthropic works. She wanted to see him and to thank him. Ratan went to see Shrimati. Shrimati employed him as a teacher for Lakhia, an orphan in her house. Shrimati refused to hear any refusal. Ratan, the 'unemployed loafer', got an employment, and became a decent man in a decent society.

Days passed. Shrimati worked hard and Ratan was there—a friend whom she could talk to. But Ratan was unhappy. He was afraid of love and the day he realized that to Shrimati he was growing to be a necessity and he himself was in love with her and was pining for the unattainable, he left Shrimati's place. The vagabond took to the streets again and the woman took to the manly duties of a public life because she had lost her private one.

Time and tide wait for none. In silent anguish Shrimati suffered, for she wanted to live, to love, to have a home, to have children. She relentlessly fought with her own self, but her mental stamina eventually gave way. She vanished away from among the crowd in dead silence, forsaking the dreamland she created for herself in the hope of a brighter morrow. She had bequeathed everything to Lakhia with a request to carry on the institution. She also left a personal letter for Ratan.

Far, far away from the din and bustle of humanity, in a lonely cottage lived Shrimati nursing her broken heart. She was on her way to the grave. She was waiting for the man who could understand her. She wanted the man by her side at her deathbed who would shed a drop of tear for her and who would help her to pass into the great Beyond. Did Ratan come back and sing her to sleep—the Sleep of Eternity?

Lagan

The Principal (played by Nemo) of a Music College for girls, quite pleased with himself for the arrangements made for the annual social, finds his apple-cart upset at the eleventh hour; not knowing what to do, he is at his wit's end when, contrary to expectations, Kusum Kumari, (played by Kanan) a student of the college, much against the Principal's wishes, plays a gramophone-record, which astonishingly solves the knotty problem. As an unknown and unacclaimed poet is the composer of the beautiful song. The ever-alert Principal seizes the opportunity and brings this poet (played by Saigal) from his native village. The poet rents a room in a mansion where incidentally, Kusum Kumari, who is indirectly responsible for his job, occupies the top floor.

The poet chooses Kusum Kumari to sing at the annual social of Music College, and coaches her.

Kusum Kumari justifies the selection and progresses to the full satisfaction of her tutor.

Tutor and pupil spend many hours together practising and rehearsing in an effort to put up a fine performance at the social. Subconsciously the poet is being drawn closer and closer by the magnetic charm of this beautiful and talented girl.

The annual event comes off very successfully. Praises and honours are showered upon the girl. The poet goes unrecognized. He is pushed into the background. The impulsive and eccentric though talented poet receives a serious shock. He is ignored. He departs.

The President of the function is a middle-aged, highly successful unmarried businessman (played by Nawab). In his attempt to gain fame and wealth, he had found no time for anything but his work. He is on the top of the world now and, for the first time in his life, he is more attracted by the melodious voice and singing, than by the beauty of this talented girl. He falls headlong into love with her. He desires to marry her. The Principal of the Music College makes the necessary arrangements. The father (played by Jagdish) of the girl is very pleased with the proposal, for after all one of the richest and most powerful men of city would be his son-in-law. He accepts. The marriage is arranged. The eccentric and selfish poet hears of the coming event. He rushes back. He protests vehemently, and in the protests, he bursts out with his ardent love for the girl. The girl is painfully surprised. She had loved and respected him as her tutor and guide. The poet is frantic. What does the girl do? What can she do?

The marriage takes place. The girl lives like a queen. The husband adores her. Is the girl happy or is she like a bird in a gilded cage? The husband senses that something is missing to complete her happiness. The girl confides in her husband. She misses her tutor—the tutor to whom she owes her present position. The comforts and joys which are hers now are the direct outcome of his efforts, and he may be rotting somewhere, without clothes, without recognition. She tells her husband that she had written to the poet but letters had returned unopened. She could not trace him. The husband promises to find the poet. He must complete his beloved's happiness. He must give the poet all the name and fame he deserves. He moves Heaven and Earth. The poet is found. He is acclaimed. He is honoured and pushed to the top by the husband.

The girl is happy. The husband is happier. The poet misunderstands. He misinterprets the girls's motive. The old flame is rekindled. The misguided poet claims her. The girl dissuades him. Reason does not appeal to him. Love has driven him mad. He must have her. For a moment the husband misunderstands; she misunderstands her husband. The situation is tense. Three lives are hanging in the balance; she loves him who loves her not, and he loves her who love him not—what a tangle!

Bhakt Surdas

Ramdas's son Bilwamangal was a Brahmin by birth but he was a poet by *karma*. He was in search of one who could sing his poems revealing their beauty and charm and please him. He met Chintamani, the bewitching professional songstress of the town, whose soulful singing made him feel that his dreams had come true. He was so captivated by her art that he forgot his old father and his wife Rambha. And Chintamani fell in love with his poetic charms. Such fascination for each other's art kept them together day in and day out.

Once Bilwamangal asked Rambha what she thought of him and the devout wife replied that, to her, his happiness was always the source of satisfaction and pleasure. He gave no ear to his father's threats and abuses of the society. Chintamani's mother tried to persuade her that singing was her business and a thing like love had no existence in her life, but she refused to follow the advice. Both of them were shown the door by their parents.

Lord Krishna and Narada saw them and Narada was sorry for the degeneration of the Brahmin, but Lord Krishna replied that he will be enlightened by the very cause for which he had pitied him.

One night, in the midst of Chintamani's singing, the strings of her *veena* were broken. At the very moment Ramdas died. Though there was a great storm raging outside, Bilwamangal went out to bring new strings for the *veena*. In his absence came Rambha, who requested Chintamani and obtained her promise to send Bilwamangal home to perform the funeral ceremony of his father. When Bilwamangal returned he found that the doors were closed. He took a long snake that was hanging by the window for a rope and with its help entered the room. Chintamani came to know about this and told him, 'If you had loved God so dearly . . .'

The shock of the father's death followed by the enlightening words of Chintamani opened his eyes. He renounced the worldly pleasures and decided there and then to meet Lord Krishna and remain at his feet, ever after. He travelled from place to place singing His praises. One day he met an old man who was asking for a man's heart in the name of Lord Krishna. Bilwamangal, then known as Surdas, cut open his chest and gave him his heart. Little did he know that Lord Krishna had tested His devotee in this way!

And Surdas walked on and on. He came to a city where he saw a beautiful woman, whom he followed to her house, believing that she was Chintamani. But he found that his eyes had cheated him. 'If I were blind,' he thought, 'I would not have thus been lured by beauty.' With the thought came the decision and the action followed it. He left the house as a blind man. Chintamani was worshipping his idol and instinct gave her this news. She took a vow to keep her eyes closed.

And now, Surdas was a true devotee of Lord Krishna, who had to keep His eternal promise of being at the service of his *bhakta*. He did keep it. He saved Surdas from various difficulties and helped him to fulfil his vow of composing 1,25,000 hymns.

Accompanied by Lord Krishna, Surdas started for Vrija. On the way he met his wife Rambha. He blessed her. Chintamani came to worship him and put the dust of his feet on her head. He called her his '*Guru*'.

And they reached Vrija. Here, the people were most pleasantly surprised when they saw Lord Krishna and Surdas . . .

Tansen

A great love-story of a Great Master.

Who has not heard the Great Name of Tansen, the Greatest Musical Genius of India?

As an orphan boy, Tansen was brought up by an aged Mohameddan, himself a poor but kind man.

Finding in the boy natural musical talent, the old guardian got him properly trained in one of the multifarious musical schools then prevalent in India.

Though Tansen quickly mastered the art that was taught to him, it was left to a shepherd girl, Tani, to show to him that rhythm did play an important part in music. And soon Tansen found that it was not the analysis but synthesis of human voice that made music—though contrary were the opinions of the different schools of music then extant.

Tansen, since then, devoted himself to gain proficiency in rhythmic music and also domain over the heart of Tani. To Tansen, music and Tani became synoynmous.

Through the powers of his music Tansen succeeded in taming a mad elephant of Bundelkhand and thus won the patronage of the Raja of that country.

During this time Emperor Akbar had already collected eight talented men of diverse Sciences and Arts and was searching for a ninth genius to complete his Nine Gems or 'Ratnas'. His scouts came to Bundelkhand and found Tansen, who was accepted as the Ninth 'Ratna' for the Darbar of Emperor Akbar. Tansen went to Agra. Tani followed.

Believing that Tani's love would prove a handicap rather than a help to the genius of Tansen, Emperor Akbar persuaded Tani to leave Tansen and Agra. Wise as she was, she saw the wisdom in the Emperor's advice and she left Agra so that Tansen would be great.

But Tani was the real inspiration of Tansen. Deprived of Tani he felt like a broken reed. He ceased singing altogether—even before the Emperor.

In the meantime, the Emperor's daughter fell ill. She was very fond of music, and nothing but music would appease her agony. But none but Tansen's music would please her, and Tansen had given up singing. However, after a great deal of persuasion Tansen was made to consent to sing before the princess one 'raga.' Tansen sang the 'Deepak Raga'. This 'raga' enkindled the latent fire in his body.

Suffering from this strange malady of inflamed passion, Tansen could not stay in Delhi, and he wandered here and there, ill and dying of unquenchable internal heat.

At last, he arrived where Tani was.

Tansen wanted to die at the feet of his beloved Tani who diagnosed the malady, and saw in the melody of 'Malhaar' the only specific for cure.

What music had done, music can undo—and Tansen was cured. And to this day this union dominates wherever Indian music chastens the atmosphere.

My Sister

A crash! A boy runs and gets into a room of a dilapidated house. Ramesh, a village school master, is seen there reading. The boy informs Ramesh that his sister Bimala is seriously injured by a fall. Ramesh must attend to her at once.

Ramesh finds his sister bleeding profusely. She is removed to a hospital.

She needs blood transfusion. Ramesh is prepared, but his blood is found unsuitable for the purpose.

Blood can be bought but Ramesh has no means to buy it.

A physician offers his blood. Ramesh's sister is saved.

Ramesh thanks the physician. The physician says that there is no need of any thanks. One must be prepared to do his or her bit for the other and thereby all can benefit.

Ramesh lives mainly for his sister. He has nobody else to call his own but Shankar, his friend. Shankar feels for Ramesh, who had big ambitions in life—but all ended in his being mere schoolmaster.

Ramesh is teaching in the classroom. He finds one of the boys inattentive. Ramu—the boy is being called from outside by somebody. Ramesh goes out and finds the caller nobody but Krishna, the local zamindar's daughter. Ramesh sees her, likes her and wishes that she comes again and then again to call Ramu, her cousin-brother. Ramesh and Krishna meets again. Each likes the other. Is it love?

Ramesh becomes Krishna's tutor. The zamindar finds out that Ramesh is more than a tutor to his daughter. He feels irritated but ultimately decides to marry her to Ramesh—on condition that Ramesh would live with him.

Ramesh refuses this humiliating offer and tells the zamindar that if he can earn enough some day he would come back and ask for his daughter's hand.

Ramesh goes to Calcutta. Shankar advises him to join the Metropolitan Opera Co. and get rich quickly. At first Ramesh refuses to sell his talent of singing—but ultimately he sees the Manager of the Opera Co. He is asked to see the Manager next day at an appointed time. The day after, while going to the Opera Co., he meets the doctor who saved his sister's life and is late in reaching the Opera Company's Office. The Manager is on the point of turning him out—but Rekha, a famous singer of the stage, requests the Manager to take Ramesh in. Ramesh gets a job and is grateful to Rekha. She, in her turn, falls in love with Ramesh.

Krishna comes to Calcutta and chances to see Ramesh with a lady in a car. She misunderstands and goes back. Ramesh is mortified at Krishna's conduct. He thinks he will forget her for good.

Ramesh resigns from the Opera Co., the moment he hears the gossip that it is only because of Rekha's favour that he is in his job.

Alarm signal blows in the city. Everything is topsy-turvy. Everybody is panicky, Ramesh finds it difficult to find a job at this crisis. Meantime Rekha again requests the Opera Co. to take back Ramesh—but the Manager is doubtful about his coming back and rejoining.

Krishna is pining at her village home. The zamindar feels worried. He comes to Calcutta to see Ramesh. He finds an assemblage of creditors at his place—and Ramesh's sister. Ramesh was out. The zamindar talks to the sister and accuses her of being the root of all troubles for Ramesh. The girl understands everything.

Ramesh comes back home, but finds his sister missing.

The siren goes again. Calcutta is bombed. Ramesh is injured. After recovery he is taken to his flat from the hospital. Shankar requests Ramesh to leave the city. He refuses.

A telegram from the village. Ramesh's sister is seriously ill. Ramesh rushes to the village and finds Bimala at the zamindar's place.

Ramesh is surprised: Does this mean a total change in the life of Ramesh? Does this mean the end of all misunderstanding between the two lovers?

The screen gives the answers to all the above questions and in a manner to make you happy.

Tadbir

Dr Kannahyalal was a very generous-hearted and pious man and yet from the day of his birth, fate had been unkind to him. In fact his life was nothing but a struggle against the evil fate.

His father, Seth Bansilal was a rich businessman and an owner of a chemical factory. When his second wife Parvati, gave birth to a child on an ill-fated day he got a horoscope made for his son and showed it to the astrologer. With great reluctance, the astrologer told his prediction to the effect that if this son lives, he will bring disaster to the family and its wealth and when he grows up he will go after a prostitute, learn to use a knife and end his life on the gallows.

After hearing this terrible forecast, Jwala Prasad, the step-brother of Kannahyalal requested his father that since the newly born son is destined to bring disaster for the family, it would be better to end his life by drowning him in milk as was the custom in the days of Rajputs [sic]. But before Seth Bansilal could make any decision, Parvati intervened and said that the destiny of a son is determined by the way he is brought up by his mother and she assured her husband that by her training she will see that her son will grow into a truly noble and honest youth.

But while Parvati started giving him the right type of training, Kannahyalal's evil fate wrought a havoc, thanks to manipulations of Jwala Prasad. Bansilal committed suicide; and an attempt was made by Jwala Prasad's henchmen to murder unlucky Kannahyalal. But thanks to the intervention of the blind old servant Bharatram, the child was saved and Parvati ran away with him from the place. But ill-luck pursued them and ultimately the widowed mother and child sought refuge in a prostitute Saguna's house. The prostitute became the virtual mother and Parvati remained a maid servant. In the new environment Kannahyalal had all the bad company which ruins a boy's life; and to the best of her ability Parvati tried to lead him on the right path by counteracting the evil influence of other children with her pious education.

But unfortunately, the ill-luck of Kannahyalal pursued him even there too. Jwala Prasad tried once again to get rid of his step-brother; but Saguna at the cost of her own life saved Kannahyalal. The crooked brain of Jwala Prasad succeeded in shifting the blame on Parvati Devi who was sentenced by the Court for twenty years life imprisonment.

Though deprived of all motherly protection. Kannahyalal remembered his mother's teachings. He never spoke a lie; never ate anything unless he could give a piece of it to a needy human being. With determined effort, he grew up into an ideal citizen and he learnt to use the knife not to kill people but save them from death.

The old servant Bharatram, his two daughters, Nirmala and Sushila, who was a widow, were Kannahyalal's friends and relations in life.

When Bharatram proposed that Kannahyalal marry Nirmala and when Kannahyalal became a doctor, he thought that at last destiny had begun to smile on him. Little did he know then that fate was planning a new disaster to test his integrity through the evil hands of Jwala Prasad. Here at last his honesty and truthfulness and his culture and education were put to an acid test. How he faced this test and how his pious deeds saved him from the gallows form the thrilling climax to this dramatic story of human struggle and can be best appreciated on the screen.

*F*ilmindia was the foremost leading film magazine in the country during the 1930s and 1940s. The film reviews published in it were widely read by film makers and cinemagoers. In a way they had some influence on the box-office prospects of the films so covered.

Dushman

Love laughs at prison bars and from time immemorial the greater the obstacles in the way of true love the greater has been the zeal with which young lovers have loved! Who has yet met the young lover who has not scoffed at poverty, tribulations, failures and social hurdles? Mohan the humble young radio-singer was no exception to the rule and dreamt happily and without restriction of the day when he and the girl of his choice—Gita—the beautiful and only child of Rai Bahadur Hiralal, would be united. That Gita returned Mohan's affections there was no doubt and her doting father was secretly well content to allow his daughter to ultimately choose a mate to her own liking, but Gita's mother, typical of society mothers throughout the world, had plans of her own and frowned on Gita's friendship with Mohan. Her choice of a fit consort for her daughter was Dr Kedar, the rising young physician of the town.

The course of true love never does run smooth—and perhaps due to Mohan's poverty, as also to his irregular habits, nature took a hand in the game by causing Mohan's health to deteriorate. This was as good an excuse as any for the mother to raise serious and effective objection to Gita's matrimonial leanings.

Frantic with worry and the prospect of his romance being broken, Mohan, after consulting Gita, rushes to his best friend Dr Kedar for medical advice. Not knowing the direction in which Mohan's affections lay, Dr Kedar advises him discreetly not to marry for one year at least. Only to divert Mohan's mind from the obvious shock at such advice, he unthinkingly suggests that Mohan should accompany him to tea at the house of the girl to whom he is shortly to be affianced.

Thus fate plays its most cruel joke on the two friends and Mohan, when he realizes that it is Gita to whom his friend is going to be engaged, releases her from her promise to him, notwithstanding her tearful and vehement protests—and like a wounded animal in agony, effaces himself from his circle of friends and goes into the distant country.

These worries tell further on Mohan's health and the continual brooding assists yet another enemy which is always lurking round the corner to catch the unwary and the careless, the underfed and the struggling—and Mohan is discovered by the workers of a humble sanatorium to be in the first stage of a dreaded disease.

With the true spirit of a good samaritan, the doctor in charge of the sanatorium compels Mohan, who does not want to live, to enter the sanatorium for a cure.

In the meantime Mohan is taken for dead amongst his circle of friends, and Gita, in despair and through continual pressure, finally agrees to her marriage with Dr Kedar. As the date of the marriage draws near, fate once again takes a hand in the shape of a countrywide appeal for the support of and the creation of more sanatoria throughout India. Mohan now cured and staying as a worker in the sanatorium (to which he had been originally taken against his will) gladly lends his services to this movement by agreeing to sing for a broadcast programme to be relayed from the sanatorium. On the other side Dr Kedar is also doing his bit by organizing a charity show in which Gita is to dance. The fateful day set for the All India Tuberculosis appeal finds the show about to start when Gita hears Mohan's voice on the radio and realizes that he is alive. Pent up with emotion she goes through her dance and collapses at the end of it, and Dr Kedar ascribes this collapse to strain. But a mutual friend who knows both Mohan and Gita ascribes it to

Gita's knowledge that Mohan was alive and betrays the fact that Gita was the girl for whose hand Mohan had always dreamt.

Recovering consciousness in her house, Gita accidentally comes to know Mohan's whereabouts and slips away from the house in her car. The family discovers her absence and telephones Dr Kedar who, guessing Gita's probable destination, rushes after her in his car in order to be near her lest there be another collapse.

Gita realizes Dr Kedar is following her and, misinterpreting his intentions, puts on more speed, loses control, and has a crash when she is very near the sanatorium where Mohan lives and works.

Thus it is that the three of them are brought together once again, with Gita lying unconscious and with each man in a state of mental agony wondering if Gita will live and then wondering that if she did, who would be her choice.

We leave you, dear patron, now to discover for yourself the answers to these two agonizing questions.

The name 'Dushman' is clearly an afterthought. The producers must be having good reasons to name this straight and simple love yarn thus and throw on it a transparent shadow of propaganda. It is whispered that the picture is an anti-tuberculosis propaganda, subtly portrayed to make it merely suggestive and thus more instructive, undertaken at the request of Lady Linlithgow. Having no evidence to the contrary we believe it is a carefully organized rumour, but fail to find much of the 'supposed subtle propaganda' in the picture. A couple of scenes, where the talk is a bit prolonged, admit some tuberculosis 'germs' into the story, but beyond that the picture doesn't suffer from either pulmonary or any other type of tuberculosis.

Acting: For the first time I saw Saigal acting and liked him for it. In several places he has given polished work. Now that our most melodious singer has started to act we can look forward to some really good work from him in future. Leela Desai must spend a little more time with her diction. She didn't come to my expectations in her work, but her portrayal being cleverly based on her native drawbacks, impressed well in the frivolous moments of the story. Her dance, however, was very good. It had more purpose than school and is beautifully developed to the emotional frenzy so dramatically portrayed and needed in the scene. The sound behind Leela's song sounded like Kamla Jharia's. Lip synchronization was correct, but an action of the hand gave it away. Najam didn't impress me, as the direction in his work looked obvious. Nemo and Deobala proved what really good artistes with experience can do. Jagdish and Prithviraj had very little to do and they did it well as usual.

Production: Clever Scenario—Masterly Direction—Beautiful Photography—Good Music—But Common Story! These are some of the outstanding impressions left behind by the picture. No one but Nitin Bose with his camera creating sequences and situations from foot to foot, could make a picture out of this thin story. Nitin's camera has created this picture throughout and that is why it has become a pictorial poem which suffers no forced accommodation for the TB 'germs'.

One shot however needs a retake and that is the first studio shot of the motor, where the studio dummy does not show the finish of the real one. It would be all right for an Andheri studio to risk a crude shot like that, but not for New Theatres.

The picture has only four songs, absolutely incidental and necessary, and they are all good. Dialogues are well written. The sets were attractive and particularly the staircase set. It looked solid and didn't suffer from 'nerves'.

The cleverest touch in the treatment of the story is the return of Gita with Dr Kedar to the scene of her love frolics with Mohan, where the vagrant musician plays on his fiddle. By rehearsing the same scenes with another man, she opens the old wounds again in an attempt to increase her soul resistance and forget the old ache, but breaks down when the pathetic note from the violin suddenly stabs her heart and wakes up the dormant emotions. This subtle, psychological scene takes Nitin a lot up in the estimate of the intellectuals.

Point of Appeal: If one is not misled by the name 'Dushman' he has no reason to be disappointed if he does not find the 'TB' in it. The picture presents a good romantic and interesting story and should be seen because of New Theatres. An excellent entertainment!

Zindagi is Poor Life

Beautiful Singing Sustains Audience Interest!

This story of two vagabonds itself becomes a vagabond picture wandering away from time-worn methods of story development into strange channels of psychological phantasies and leaving the audience vagabonding to find what it is all about.

It is debatable wheter the high-flown treatment which is given to the photoplay, with its ultimate barren conclusion, will be popularly acceptable to the people in general.

For harnessing ideological fancies to entertainment, it is necessary that those responsible for the production of such pictures should bring the subject within the intellectual limits of the masses. For, unless the picture is a success at the box-offices, its intended effect on the public is nil.

The story has hardly any important incidents except several sequences of psychological dissimulations which leave even an intellectual bored.

The memory one takes of the picture is the last song of Saigal *Soja, soja, raj kumari*. The rest is smoke.

The principal fault is the selection of suc a subject with its obscure design of misty ideology for a photoplay.

Forgetting this fundamental defect for a while, the picture is marvellously directed and beautifully photographed.

Jamuna, whose lasting dignity few women can equal, gives a supreme performance which because of its excellence people tolerate in an otherwise boring picture.

What Saigal sings is music and when the golden notes come out of his throat, people forget the story writer, the director, the producer and even Saigal's big face monopolizing the screen for a long time. They just want his maddening music and there is a good amount of it in this picture.

If this picture runs a long time it will be because Saigal has sung beautifully and not because Barua has directed it.

Lagan

Orthodox Story and Boring Picture

Nitin's *Lagan* is certainly a better picture than *Har Jeet* and *Andhi* but it is too poor in comparison with his own *Dushman* and nothing to write home about considering the old standard of New Theatres.

Whatever might have been the state of confusion in the New Theatres Studio, one expected Nitin Bose to give at least a technically superb picture. The fact that he has not been able to do so, after nearly a year on *Lagan*, proves the necessity of a radical overhaul in the studio organization.

The story of *Lagan* is orthodox and insipid and seems to have stepped out of an obsolete story book. It is the story of a music teacher, charitably called a poet, and a disciple, whom we are supposed to take as a young girl in spite of her size and proportions.

There are some blind fools in the town who think *Lagan* to be a great picture. Yes, it is certainly great in comparison with *Andhi*. But for Nitin Bose, it is a damn poor show. Nitin must not be misguided by the phrases of the publicity pups nor pat himself on the back by reading readymade reviews appearing in the dailies.

We are prepared to lose *Lagan* but losing Nitin will be a tragedy. Nitin must give us a really great picture. It is in him to make one. If New Theatres won't give him the facilities, let him go out and make it but his next one must be even better than *Dushman*. In the meanwhile, let him remember that *Lagan* is a setback to his reputation as a great director but let that not dishearten him towards greater effort.

Coming to *Lagan*, its photography is indifferent. A couple of songs are good, but as the music is inclined to be on classic lines it fails to be popular.

Kanan gives a pretty good performance and sings a song well. Saigal does not impress. Nemo is tiresome and so is Jagdish who hasn't much to do. Nawab fails even to amuse.

The story is loosely knit and becomes boring in places. During the last four reels it however rushes well. But that is all.

As I said before, there is nothing much to crow about, whatever hired pups might say.

Bhakt Surdas Draws Huge Crowds

The story or Surdas is known to all. It has always provided a popular social plot to stage and screen writers and it has always drawn crowds of the devotionally minded people.

On the stage—Hindi, Gujarati and Marathi—Surdas has become a classic and as such has always appealed to people, though the story development has been common throughout different languages.

Ranjit, probably, wanted to be different from these popularly accepted versions and in consequence has made a feeble attempt to give a new complexion to the story, especially by giving it a socially progressive trend. While in conception, the Ranjit attempt is praiseworthy, in actual execution it is rather a poor effort.

The main objection is to be found in the irreverent and frivolous portrayal of Surdas in the first half of the picture.

Ranjit's Bilwamangal looks like an erratic playboy of 1942 indulging frivolously in sex-play and not a budding poet whose lyrics were destined to be immortal.

Bilwamangal who was born to be great as poet and sant Surdas, even realizing that his early life presented a sharp contrast by his indulgence in physical pleasures of life, could not have stooped so low as to be a cheap modern womanizer that he has been shown to be. Even in his carnal desires and passions he would be expected to display a dignified restraint so characteristic of the old times when love had a more dignified and subdued technique of expression.

To see Ranjit's Bilwamangal dancing round the terrace holding Chintamani's hand like an overgrown schoolboy rather outrages our emotional conceptions of love in the old times.

The men who portrayed this character in the present frivolous strain, should only recall the intimate relations between their own parents to realize how conservative and dignified must have been the old lovers' ways in the expression of their emotions.

Not a Modern Prostitute

Chintamani, the professional songstress, has become an immortal character because she inspired Bilwamangal to take the path of devotion, thus giving his lyrics a divine mission.

Prostitution is as old an institution as humanity and prostitutes have gone through different evolutions and transformations through the ages. Chintamani was not the type to be compared with our modern singing girls found in Hira Mandis and Chowri Bazaars. She was more fashioned after the famous courtesans of history like Mahananda, Vasantasena and others. Her approach, therefore, to her hereditary profession was more dignified and though acquiring wealth has been the underlying design for the prostitute's pattern of life, the prostitute of old put more grace and less frivolity in her trade. History reveals names of prostitutes who have been revered through ages. Chintamani belonged to this class and to show her indulging in childish and frivolous skipping on the terrace with Bilwamangal, which director Chaturbhuj Doshi has made her do, at once becomes unconvincing and revolting.

Production values in the picture are too poor for Ranjit. The sound recording is not all that it should have been and the photography is definitely poor.

Once before, I had written that the technical work in recent Ranjit pictures has been degenerating consistently. *Surdas* provides another evidence in support of my previous statement.

The direction of Chaturbhuj Doshi, to say the least, is completely unimaginative and dissatisfactory. In the early half of the picture he has given his main characters modern modes of behaviour and thus made them look frivolous and ridiculous.

In the latter half, a scene like Bilwamangal climbing up a serpent, which is a time-honoured highlight of the story, goes unnoticed because the director fails to bring the audience to a pitch of suspense and anxiety.

Likewise, the scene in which Chintamani inspires Bilwamangal to give up his old ways, though the scene is the most important key situation in the story, runs through the picture with the least pretensions of any deep human emotions. That scene completely fails.

It is, however, true that some deep pathos incidental to a few naturally pathetic situations in the latter half of the picture helps the audience to be moved to tears and thus one feels a lot compensated for the unexpected frivolity pervading throughout the early part of the picture.

But after scrutinizing carefully the director's work, I still felt that the psychological and philosophical demands of the theme went right over the head of the director and when certain inherently emotional situations banged him on the head at times, he clean ducked himself out of them. That is not much to speak for an intellectual like Chaturbhuj Doshi, who had been given a chance of a lifetime to prove his ability as a director by being given a popular subject and stars like Saigal and Khurshid to crowd the box-offices.

Barring the original lyrics of *Surdas*, every other song is too badly written by Madhok. Madhok seems to lack the elevating glow of Hindu culture which is so essential in choosing the right words for the theme and the age of the story. Dialogues, however, are good in parts.

With Saigal and Khurshid leading the cast, one expected a feast of real music in *Surdas*.

In spite of several tunes being not attractive, when Saigal sings them music floats in the air and for the time being one cannot help but be charmed. Saigal's acting, however, which was never much before, is much less in this picture.

Khurshid—poor girl—she has suffered because of the director. She is known to give good work usually, but, probably, she was not asked to do so in this picture.

The best performance in the picture is given by Monica Desai. She has a very sympathetic role to play in the mould of the traditional Hindu wife of Surdas, and she does full justice to it.

Nagendra becomes unnecessarily melodramatic at places.

Well, *Surdas* will still pull very well at the box-offices, because even director Chaturbhuj Doshi can not make *Surdas* unpopular, the way he has made a home in very Hindu heart through generations.

My Sister, a Common Story Clumsily Done

This is a propaganda story produced for the Government of India in the hope that, after showing it, people will rush to deposit their blood in the blood banks of the country. Actually by the time you come to the end, all about the blood and the blood bank is completely forgotten and the purpose of the production stands entirely frustrated by the time we see the last foot of the picture.

Forgetting the propaganda angle about the blood bank, the story is about a brother's love for his little sister. As such, it is stretched a bit to meet the demands of the orthodox minds.

Throughout the picture there is neither a single novelty nor a single twist which would take any praise or admiration.

At the end of it all, the hero gets the heroine and he finds his sister also in the heroine's house. This ends the usual orthodox humbug. From the beginning to the end the story part of *My Sister* remains flimsy and unconvincing.

The direction of Hem Chunder is far from satisfactory and certainly not up to the standard which he attained in *Wapas*. Pankaj Mullick, the music-director, has dished out some old tunes by changing the opening lines. And from this affair only one tune attracts a bit. The lyrical compositions of Pundit Bhusan are rather awkward and clumsy. Sound and photography are of a mediocre standard.

From the players Saigal, old and tired as usual, this time sings with a broken reed in the throat. Sumitra who is cast as the heroine is evidently a newcomer to the screen. She wears a startled expression and though she looks pretty attractive in life, she does not maintain this impression on the screen. Beyond running about she does nothing worthy of attention. Nawab overacts as the boss of the theatrical company. Akhtar Jehan and Chandravati do nothing much to write home about in the roles of Bimla and Rekha.

There is nothing special in the picture to attract. On the other hand, it is a bit boring at places. The picture is, however, expected to run well because of its orthodox theme and just because it is produced by New Theatres who still enjoy the goodwill of the people.

Tadbir, A Jayant–Dave Jumble!

Long before anything else can happen to you in this picture, the tragedy of Saigal comes home. Years ago when the New Theatres discovered Saigal, the Indian screen secured overnight its most emotional singer with the proverbial golden voice. Saigal soon became the ambition of every musician in the country. Every young man and woman in the country crooned Saigal's famous songs and within a year over a million throats sung Saigal's popular hits in every nook and corner of India. Saigal has never been a big musician. He had only the divine gift of a glorious voice the like of which has not yet been heard on the Indian screen. We doubt whether the ever-genial Saigal ever had any enemies, but if he had some, even they could not have wished any ill to his unique voice. Saigal's voice was considered to be a nation's pride. And justly so. For years he thrilled millions and brought new music into a country that was just becoming unmusical. Saigal must have inspired thousands to learn music and no single person has contributed more to the popularity of Indian music than Saigal has done during the last two years.

But the man whom Divinity had blessed with such a rare gift proved a bad artist with his own life. He does not seem to have realized that life's greatest art is life itself. Today he croaks like a sick frog when once his incomparable melody would fill the theatre with thrilling subtleties of human emotions. Though Saigal still stumbles through a weary existence, he is really dead. No longer do we see in him that little spark of Divinity which had given this man a glorious opportunity to entertain a willing nation of millions. Saigal is dead. But his song will live for many more years till we get another Saigal.

Coming to the picture, we find that this fellow Jayant Desai seems to be a very unreliable guy. In *Chandragupta* he had shown definite signs of improvement not only in the technique of production but also in harnessing the motion picture for some purpose.

In *Tadbir*, he seems to have gone back to his old game of cheap, inconsequential stuff to woo the masses.

Tadbir is a story in which there is enough material for fifty more stories. In almost every reel there are at least four such situations on which a full-length screenplay can be easily written. Logic and reason usually never strike Jayant Desai and such a possibility is very remote when Mohanlal Dave conspires with Jayant to give us a picture.

The production values of the picture are rather hurried and crude. The music is not happy. Sound and photography are indifferent throughout. Almost every item of production seems to be a clumsy job done in an unholy hurry. The direction is far from being suitable or satisfactory.

From the players, Mubarak has given an excellent performance in the very sympathetic role of Bharatram, the blind servant. One wishes, however, that his make-up had shown some age with the years skipped through in the story. It seems Bharatram had a rare gift of good health and looked the same even after a lapse of twenty years. In any case Mubarak's good performance is very welcome after a long time.

Saigal is asked to play the role of a twenty-four-year-old medico. He looks exactly double the age in the role of Dr Kanhaiyalal. The poor fellow tries to act but most of the time he seems to drag his half-dead body. What he sings is no longer music.

Suraiya is not at all bad as Nirmala, the heroine of the story, while Salvi does justice to his role of the villain in the traditional manner. From the rest Jiloobai does very well as Parvati, the mother of Kanhaiyalal, though at times she over-acts terribly.

Well, *Tadbir* is tolerable in parts if you don't look the gift-horse too closely in the mouth. After the interval the story succeeds in gaining some grip which helps to keep the spectators in the chair much against their will.

Kardar Gives India's Best Historical Picture!

Shah Jehan, a Beautiful Tribute to the Taj!

We had always suspected Kardar of being a rare artist, in spite of the several indifferent motion pictures given by him recently.

After seeing *Shah Jehan*, his latest artistic creation, at a special show, we unhesitatingly pronounce him as the most artistic director of India, a man whose delicate and superb art makes seasoned professionals like Shantaram and Mehboob look like clumsy amateurs.

With a single picture Kardar has left the 'great' Shantaram at least a hundred years behind in almost all aspects of motion picture production. Kardar's *Shah Jehan* severely competes with Hollywood's imposing technique and quality and one can't help but muse whether even Hollywood producers, with their vast resources, could have given a more beautiful and thorough picture than *Shah Jehan* on the immortal story of the Taj.

As it stands Kardar's *Shah Jehan* is perhaps the most glorious tribute any motion picture producer has yet paid to love's most pathetic tear which froze itself into an immortal marble monument.

Shah Jehan is easily the best historical picture produced in our country during the last thirty years. And before that we had no film industry. And because of its rare quality, exceptional in the Indian film industry, *Shah Jehan* belongs more to the nation than to the individual who produced it. And as such, this picture should be sent overseas not only as a convincing evidence of our film art, but as an eloquent proof of the glory that was India.

The beauty of *Shah Jehan* is a proof of the harmony and cooperation between the different technicians. Art director M.R. Achrekar, a well-known artist of India, takes us back to the good old days of Moghul glory when emperors were themselves artists and poets and expressed their love for finer arts by building beautiful mausoleums and writing rare emotional poetry. The sets of *Shah Jehan* are almost as great an art as the originals built by the Moghul emperors of old.

Not to be outdone by his technical colleagues, music director

Naushad, whose harmonious orchestration we have often praised, goes one better in this great picture by giving appropriate and psychologically correct mood-music, both in songs and background, which helps to intensify the emotional theme of the story considerably.

And then there is Abdul Rashid Kardar—the artistic soul of *Shah Jehan*. It is his picture and he is there in it, in every foot of it. Giving to his players a beautiful tongue with choice words, he has given them a realistic atmosphere to play their roles. Shot by shot, Kardar has built up the picture with extreme care, both technically and emotionally. In direction, this is the best work Kardar has given so far and he deserves all praise for the clever way in which he has developed his story on the screen.

Actually *Shah Jehan* has very little of history in it. It is a romance with an authentic historical atmosphere. A lot of creative imagination has been used to make up the story of *Shah Jehan* but nowhere has the producer distorted any events out of recognition and presented anything revolting.

The only criticism we have to offer is about Nasreen, in the role of Roohi. In the story Kardar works up a dramatic suspense to introduce the beautiful Roohi. But actually when he introduces Nasreen the beauty of Roohi disappears within a moment. Nasreen's face does not support Kardar's dramatic development. Nasreen has too ordinary a face to be classed as strikingly beautiful. And 'strikingly beautiful' was the demand of the story. Nasreen's work is rather poor and she remains stiff and camera-conscious throughout. Besides, she adds the Punjabi accent to her Urdu dialogue and that is not a good accent to a beautiful language.

To sum it all up, *Shah Jehan* is a picture that should be the pride of our film industry and all congratulations to producer Kardar for giving us the best historical picture in thirty years.

Parwana Presents An Erratic Story!

Saigal's Music Sustains Interest!

There are two good things about this picture: the singing of Saigal and the technical direction of Nanda despite poor story material. The rest of it is commonplace stuff including the usual Madhok songs which constitute neither music nor poetry. This time, additionally, the story is also by Madhok. You can, therefore, imagine the rut of entertainment presented.

The theme of the story is confused. It seems to be a result of muddled thinking. At places one feels that the writer is trying to argue against parent-arranged marriages. In spots, through Roopa, the wife of the hero, the writer almost screams against blind unreasonable jealousy in married life. Then there is the socialistic temperament of the hero when he befriends a beggar girl. And the communal angle when the Hindu hero loves the Muslim beggar girl as his sister. Add to these the different and temporary facets of brotherly, manly, sisterly and 'sweetheartly' love between the hero and the heroine (Gopi) and imagine the unholy mess in which the writer has presented the story on the screen.

In this erratic and idiotic design of the story are woven psychologically contradictory characters like Gopi, Roopa, Inder and Kishen. These main characters do not have any psychological consistency in the development of their roles with the result that they keep on doing odd things at odd times, wrenching off many actions from their previous psychological contexts.

In fact no one in the picture gets any sympathy except the late Mr Saigal—and that too for his premature death and not for his work in this picture.

The picture fails to appeal because of its thin and erratic story and wrong casting of characters. Saigal in spite of his age and sickly appearance was asked to act a young man in the twenties. It was too much of a deception for human eyes. Najma, with her rough goonda mannerisms and theatrical gestures, is hardly the type to portray the traditional gentle Hindu wife. She ruins the basic fibre of the story. For a village belle with that unbelievable amount of innocence as shown in the picture, a younger girl than Suraiya was required. The very development of Suraiya's bosom does not suffer even the slightest suggestion of innocence in the role she plays.

Not Bad Technically

Technically the picture is good in pats. For the first time in Bombay, Saigal's voice was nicely recorded, giving his voice as much youthful ring as could be given to the voice of a sick and dying man. Director

Nanda's technical direction is quite impressive, though his psychological interpretation of characters of the story remains crude and unconvincing. One can understand the sick Saigal being constantly wrapped in clothes and capped in addition, but why should the man playing his father be always found in full dress with his turban on even in his home? The picture sadly lacks the village atmosphere, though the story travels though a village. In future Nanda should be more particular about the atmosphere of his sequences, for, a motion picture to be convincing must reflect as many facets of life as possible.

Though Saigal has sung beautifully the words and sentiment of his songs are far from being noteworthy. Even the tunes of Khurshid Anwar are neither popular nor suitable for the situations. It is Saigal's glorious voice that lends a rare sigh and emotion to the songs.

From the players, Saigal, despite his illness and age, does his bit bravely and sings beautifully in the role of Inder, the hero. Najma is utterly miscast in the role of Roopa, Suraiya makes faces and bounces about in the role of Gopi but that is not screen acting. K.N. Singh fits in well as 'Kishen', the brother of the heroine but he has hardly anything to do except the last scream which turns out to be a scream of screams.

All done and said, it is Saigal's last picture and as such one should see it to wish a happy journey to a glorious singer even though he sings Madhok's nonsense.

Index

Read more in Penguin

Sahibs' India
Vignettes of the Raj

Pran Nevile

Sahibs' India is a panoramic look at the lives of the British in colonial India. Culled from Raj literature, it reveals little-known aspects of their lives and their dealings with their Indian subjects. Drawing from contemporary journals, plays and poems, the author provides wonderful descriptions of British homes and servants, their tastes and fashions, cultural idiosyncrasies, profligacy, sports, hunts and shoots, giving us, with the relaxed familiarity of the after-dinner raconteur, a flavour of the period. The book is peppered with a host of characters—astrologers, jugglers, magicians, grass-widows, the 'fishing fleet', missionaries, nautch girls, mavericks and eccentrics—who made India their home as the British turned from traders to empire-builders, and is interspersed with period photographs, paintings and sketches. This is a delightful evocation of a vanished world.

Penguin Books India
Non-fiction
Rs 299

Nautch Girls of the Raj

Pran Nevile

The much-celebrated nautch girl, extravagantly adored for both her beauty and her virtuosity, belonged to a unique class of courtesans who played a significant role in the social and cultural life of India in the eighteenth and nineteenth centuries. The nautch girl, it may be said, was no ordinary woman of pleasure—she had refined manners, a ready wit and poetry in her blood. She embodied a splendid synthesis of different cultures and dance forms—the classical and the popular—and catered to the sophisticated tastes of the elite who had the time, resources and inclination to enjoy her accomplishments.

Over the centuries female dancers have appeared in various incarnations, frequently as temple dancers dedicated to the gods, for dance is believed to have divine approval. However, historians, sociologists, novelists and chroniclers have not always done justice to the nautch girl, depicting her as either a vamp or as a showgirl bought by the wealthy for festive occasions. This book highlights the emergence of the quintessential nautch girl in the Mughal era when she reached the zenith of her talent and charisma. Her mystique continued to reign supreme during the Raj and her popularity and status among the English sahibs and the Indian aristocracy flourished during this period.

Illustrated with reproductions and drawings obtained from collections all over the world this book offers a vivid glimpse of the seductive allure and dazzling grace of nautch in its days of glory.

Penguin Books India
History
Rs 250

Read more in Penguin

Lahore
A Sentimental Journey

Pran Nevile

Lahore, first published in 1993, is Pran Nevile's tribute to the land of his birth. Grounded in memory and redolent with nostalgia, Nevile's reminiscences transport the reader into the heart of Lahore as it was in the 1930s and 40s—a city bustling with activity where people coexisted harmoniously, unfettered by considerations of religion, region or caste. From the riotous seasonal festivities of kite-flying to clandestine love-affairs upon rooftops, from matinee shows at the cinema to twilight hours spent amongst the bejewelled dancing girls of Hira Mandi, Lahore emerges as a city of mesmerizing contradictions and chaotic splendour.

The author underscores the contrast between pre- and post-Partition Lahore, and the sense of pain, loss and longing for one's homeland experienced by the displaced millions in India and Pakistan is palpable. Evocative and informative, Lahore is at once social commentary, historical documentation and memoir.

Penguin Books India
Non-fiction
Rs 250